Data Visualization with D3 and AngularJS

Build dynamic and interactive visualizations from real-world data with D3 on AngularJS

Christoph Körner

BIRMINGHAM - MUMBAI

Data Visualization with D3 and AngularJS

First published: April 2015

Production reference: 1230415

Published by Packt Publishing Ltd.
Livery Place
35 Livery Street
Birmingham B3 2PB, UK.

ISBN 978-1-78439-848-4

www.packtpub.com

Credits

Author
Christoph Körner

Reviewers
Michael Alexander
Amin Ariana
Athos Demetri
Victor Mejia
Aaron Nielsen
Jeremy Zerr

Commissioning Editor
Pramila Balan

Acquisition Editor
Shaon Basu

Content Development Editor
Akashdeep Kundu

Technical Editors
Vijin Boricha
Humera Shaikh

Copy Editor
Relin Hedly

Project Coordinator
Izzat Contractor

Proofreaders
Safis Editing
Paul Hindle

Indexer
Hemangini Bari

Graphics
Disha Haria

Production Coordinator
Nilesh R. Mohite

Cover Work
Nilesh R. Mohite

About the Author

Christoph Körner is the CTO of GESIM, a Swiss startup company, where he is responsible for its simulation software and web interface that is built using AngularJS and D3. He studied electrical engineering and information technology at Vienna University of Technology, including a 1-year exchange program at the Swiss Federal Institute of Technology, Lausanne.

Christoph is a passionate, self-taught software developer, coworker, and web enthusiast with more than 7 years of experience in designing, developing, and implementing customer-oriented web-based IT solutions. He has always been enthusiastic and curious about new technologies and started to use AngularJS and D3 since the very first version. Christoph is not only fascinated by technology, but he also aims to push cutting-edge technologies to production services.

I would like to thank my colleagues and close friends, Firat Özdemir and Vidor Kanalas, and my girlfriend, Laura Andrea Rojas Padilla, for all their input, support, and motivation during all stages of the book. I also want to offer special thanks to the whole Packt Publishing team for doing an outstanding job in supervising and supporting me.

About the Reviewers

Michael Alexander is an Australian FOSS developer who is the author of popular Angular-D3 — a D3.js directive for AngularJS. He is currently employed with HRMWEB Pty Ltd. and works on several web applications involving a range of technologies including AngularJS.

Michael also founded Miniand Pty Ltd, a company that helped the mini PC and developer board market grow in recent years in China through consultation and development directly with manufacturers.

Amin Ariana is an ex-Google and ex-Microsoft software entrepreneur in San Francisco and the cofounder and chief technology officer at Sponsorbrite Inc. He has combined the use of AngularJS and D3.js since the earliest days of their adoption at Google.

As a Carnegie Mellon University recipient of Director's Return on Education Award, Amin continues to be an ambassador of change for professionals and technology organizations alike. He combines his computer science foundations from the University of Waterloo with the disciplines of engineering, design, business, and innovation to create products and write entrepreneurial career roadmaps.

His advisory essays on scalable software engineering, entrepreneurship, innovation, and management are published in Forbes, Quora, and his personal blog at www.aminariana.com.

As the technical cofounder and CTO at Sponsorbrite, Amin leverages big data with insight-transferring solutions such as AngularJS and D3.js to bring corporate sponsorship to social institutions and communities that were left underfunded by the federal government. His team's fundraising and community relationship management platform is a prime example of how books similar to this can be tools toward multibillion-dollar social values.

Amin's upcoming book, *The Rise of The Rainmaker*, is about carving a career path from engineering to entrepreneurship. He is still writing the book and hopes to publish it digitally next year. The completed chapters of this book are accessible to members of his blog.

Special thanks to my wife, Abby Denzin, for keeping me sane enough to review this exciting book while managing a startup company and to my reviewer buddies, Izzat Contractor and Neha Thakur, for helping me reach the finish line.

Athos Demetri works as a freelance developer and technical consultant for a number of local businesses. He mostly enjoys bringing the power of the Web to technophobes. In those rare moments when he isn't working, he likes good food, yoga, techno music, cats, and enjoys laughing with friends.

I'd like to thank my mum and dad for always telling me that there's no such word as "can't" and for always being right the first time. I'd also like to thank Anja, without whose support, I'd have given up on programming years ago.

Finally, I'm also grateful to my friends for their patience and confidence in my curveball ideas about virtually everything.

Victor Mejia is a full stack web developer. He has been a part of different industries and enjoys working with full stack JavaScript and data visualization. In his spare time, you will find him coding, reading, in Bible study, and spending time with family and friends. He and his wife, Jessica, are in love and happily married. They are expecting a beautiful baby girl.

Jeremy Zerr is a web software entrepreneur and an experienced web developer, currently imparting his web application development skills to the world as a software consultant, educator, and product creator. Changing the world with well-crafted software is his passion. He writes about web development topics on his blog at `http://www.jeremyzerr.com` and offers his web software development services through his company Zerrtech at `http://www.zerrtech.com`.

www.PacktPub.com

Support files, eBooks, discount offers, and more

For support files and downloads related to your book, please visit www.PacktPub.com.

Did you know that Packt offers eBook versions of every book published, with PDF and ePub files available? You can upgrade to the eBook version at www.PacktPub.com and as a print book customer, you are entitled to a discount on the eBook copy. Get in touch with us at service@packtpub.com for more details.

At www.PacktPub.com, you can also read a collection of free technical articles, sign up for a range of free newsletters and receive exclusive discounts and offers on Packt books and eBooks.

https://www2.packtpub.com/books/subscription/packtlib

Do you need instant solutions to your IT questions? PacktLib is Packt's online digital book library. Here, you can search, access, and read Packt's entire library of books.

Why subscribe?

- Fully searchable across every book published by Packt
- Copy and paste, print, and bookmark content
- On demand and accessible via a web browser

Free access for Packt account holders

If you have an account with Packt at www.PacktPub.com, you can use this to access PacktLib today and view 9 entirely free books. Simply use your login credentials for immediate access.

Table of Contents

Preface

The question of how I could better visualize my application server's log files has always hovered around in my mind. In this book, we'll materialize this idea. After reading the book, you'll be able to analyze the log files of your application server and display them as a time series chart on a web page — a real-time autoupdating chart. I picked my two favorite JavaScript libraries — AngularJS and D3.js — to develop such a visualization.

AngularJS is a web application framework that facilitates the development of modern web applications with concepts such as the MVC/MVVM pattern, two-way data binding, testable modules, and dependency injection. I especially like the idea that one can declare templates to extend the HTML language; this enables a whole new world of applications and the sharing of work between designers and frontend engineers.

D3.js is a visualization toolkit that facilitates the generation and manipulation of web-based vector graphics with full access to the underlying SVG standard. Moreover, animations and interactive visualizations change how users perceive web applications; D3.js offers everything you need to make a visualization interactive out of the box.

In this book, I will teach you how to create an interactive real-time visualization for the Web with AngularJS as the application framework and D3.js as the visualization toolkit. I will explain the basic concepts of D3.js, when and why we use it, and why it's so much better than other DOM-transforming libraries, with a focus on its data-driven approach. Also, I will show you best practices to manipulate datasets and preprocess data — an everyday job if you want to display data from different sources. Then, we will spend more time on seeing how a visualization library can be best integrated into an AngularJS application using modules, directives, and services to make the components testable and maintainable. Later, we will focus on developing the visualization.

First, we need to load real data in the application and parse the text data to a JavaScript array of objects. Then, we need to preprocess and group the data according to the way we want to display it. Now, we can generate a curve or shape in the chart that represents our data. Next, we want to animate this curve—to show a transition between the old and the new state—whenever we update the data of the chart. We also want to zoom and pan inside the charts and create filters in order to clamp the chart to a certain range, for example, a starting time and an ending time for the time series data. Finally, we want to put everything together on to a dashboard and feed it with real server logs of a web server.

Displaying data on the web is a common task for developers. This books walks you through an exciting project, explaining best practices and common pitfalls in this domain using the two most amazing JavaScript libraries: AngularJS and D3.js.

What this book covers

Chapter 1, The Magic of SVG, D3.js, and AngularJS, introduces you to the world of vector graphics on the web and points out the advantages of D3.js.

Chapter 2, Getting Started with D3.js, explains how to draw vector graphics with D3.js and its data-driven approach.

Chapter 3, Manipulating Data, walks you through the important task of manipulating and preprocessing datasets in JavaScript and D3.js.

Chapter 4, Building a Chart Directive, lets you implement a first scatter chart directive in order to integrate the visualization into a simple AngularJS application with a focus on modularization and testability.

Chapter 5, Loading and Parsing Data, explains how to load files and parse real data using AngularJS and D3.js. It also explains how to aggregate information for the visualization.

Chapter 6, Drawing Curves and Shapes, helps you understand lines, curves, and shapes in SVG and D3.js in order to create different chart types, such as line charts, area charts, and bar charts.

Chapter 7, Controlling Transitions and Animations, shows how animations can be used to better visualize changes in the dataset and the visualization. You will learn about animations in D3.js and how to create plausible transitions to update chart directives.

Chapter 8, Bringing the Chart to Life with Interactions, explains how to add interactions to the chart directive, which is a big advantage of web-based visualizations. You will also see how to combine and encapsulate the interactions of the D3 chart and the AngularJS application.

Chapter 9, Building a Real-time Visualization to Monitor Server Logs, walks you through an exciting example where you will use all the acquired knowledge of the book to build a visualization dashboard to analyze server logs.

What you need for this book

To get started, all you need is a web browser and a text editor, such as Sublime Text. However, I recommend that you install Node.js (`http://nodejs.org/`) that includes the npm package manager and the Bower (`http://bower.io/`) module in order to run the tests. I will walk you through the installation of the required packages in the corresponding chapters.

Starting from *Chapter 4, Building a Chart Directive*, we will use the http-server module (`https://www.npmjs.com/package/http-server`) to run the examples from a local web server. An internet connection is only required for installing tools and libraries, but not for running the examples.

Who this book is for

Data Visualization with D3 and AngularJS is intended for web developers with experience in AngularJS who want to implement fully customizable interactive vector graphics for all platforms. Whether you already know a bit about SVG and vector graphics in the browser or have never used any visualization library in JavaScript before, you will be able to master the data-driven techniques of D3. In either case, this book will get you up and running quickly and also challenges you if you have already worked with D3.

Conventions

In this book, you will find a number of text styles that distinguish between different kinds of information. Here are some examples of these styles and an explanation of their meaning.

Code words in text, database table names, folder names, filenames, file extensions, pathnames, dummy URLs, user input, and Twitter handles are shown as follows: "The `.exit()` function will return all elements of the Selection because the dataset contains no elements."

A block of code is set as follows:

```html
<html>
  <head>
    <title>My App</title>
  </head>
  <body>
    <h1 class="header>My Application</h1>
    <p class="content">
      Lorem ipsum dolor sit amet, ...
    </p>
  </body>
</html>
```

When we wish to draw your attention to a particular part of a code block, the relevant lines or items are set in bold:

```html
<html>
  ...
  <body>
  <object id="vis" width="50" height="30">
    <param name="movie" value="vis.swf">
    <embed src="vis.swf" type="application/x-shockwave-flash">
  </object>
  </body>
</html>
```

Any command-line input or output is written as follows:

```
npm install --save express
npm install --save serve-static
```

New terms and **important words** are shown in bold. Words that you see on the screen, for example, in menus or dialog boxes, appear in the text like this: "The t parameter in the range 0 to 1 defines the position on the curve between the starting point P_0 (in the figure **P1**) and the end point P_3 (in the figure **P2**); P_1 (in the figure **C1**) and P_2 (in the figure **C2**) are called control points and are used to model the shape between these points."

 Warnings or important notes appear in a box like this.

 Tips and tricks appear like this.

Reader feedback

Feedback from our readers is always welcome. Let us know what you think about this book—what you liked or disliked. Reader feedback is important for us as it helps us develop titles that you will really get the most out of.

To send us general feedback, simply e-mail feedback@packtpub.com, and mention the book's title in the subject of your message.

If there is a topic that you have expertise in and you are interested in either writing or contributing to a book, see our author guide at www.packtpub.com/authors.

Customer support

Now that you are the proud owner of a Packt book, we have a number of things to help you to get the most from your purchase.

Downloading the example code

You can download the example code files from your account at http://www.packtpub.com for all the Packt Publishing books you have purchased. If you purchased this book elsewhere, you can visit http://www.packtpub.com/support and register to have the files e-mailed directly to you.

Downloading the color images of this book

We also provide you with a PDF file that has color images of the screenshots/diagrams used in this book. The color images will help you better understand the changes in the output. You can download this file from: https://www.packtpub.com/sites/default/files/downloads/8484OS_Graphics.pdf.

Errata

Although we have taken every care to ensure the accuracy of our content, mistakes do happen. If you find a mistake in one of our books—maybe a mistake in the text or the code—we would be grateful if you could report this to us. By doing so, you can save other readers from frustration and help us improve subsequent versions of this book. If you find any errata, please report them by visiting http://www.packtpub.com/submit-errata, selecting your book, clicking on the **Errata Submission Form** link, and entering the details of your errata. Once your errata are verified, your submission will be accepted and the errata will be uploaded to our website or added to any list of existing errata under the Errata section of that title.

To view the previously submitted errata, go to `https://www.packtpub.com/books/content/support` and enter the name of the book in the search field. The required information will appear under the **Errata** section.

Piracy

Piracy of copyrighted material on the Internet is an ongoing problem across all media. At Packt, we take the protection of our copyright and licenses very seriously. If you come across any illegal copies of our works in any form on the Internet, please provide us with the location address or website name immediately so that we can pursue a remedy.

Please contact us at `copyright@packtpub.com` with a link to the suspected pirated material.

We appreciate your help in protecting our authors and our ability to bring you valuable content.

Questions

If you have a problem with any aspect of this book, you can contact us at `questions@packtpub.com`, and we will do our best to address the problem.

1
The Magic of SVG, D3.js, and AngularJS

In this book, we will develop an application that combines both frameworks **D3.js** and **AngularJS** into a stunning interactive visualization, an interactive dashboard to visualize server logs in real time. First, I will discuss the outline and the purpose of this application. Then, I will explain how to modularize the visualization so that all components can be seamlessly embedded into one single application.

In the second section, we will talk about the terminology and definitions that are used in this book to introduce you to this topic or to refresh your knowledge of some basics in computer graphics. It will help you to understand why we are using vector graphics—especially **SVG** for the Web—for the visualization that we will develop in this book (and not, for example, **Canvas** or **WebGL**).

The next part of the chapter will give an introduction to D3.js and its **data-driven** approach. It will help you to understand the similarities and fundamental differences of D3.js and other DOM transforming libraries such as **jQuery**. Then, we will see an introduction to AngularJS and discuss its strengths for modern application development as well as the integration of D3.js into an AngularJS application.

The last section of this chapter will help you to understand why we prefer D3.js over other visualization libraries. It will give a brief outline and comparison of web visualization tools emphasizing on libraries to create and manipulate vector graphics and the evolution of web standards. We will discuss the main ideas and advantages of using D3.js in web applications and the differences between it and other tools for web visualizations (such as **Raphaël** or **Three.js**).

In this chapter, you will learn:

- How to distinguish vector and pixel graphics and to know their application areas
- When and why to use vector graphics, especially SVG
- Why D3.js is superior to other common graphical toolkits
- When and why to use D3.js for creating graphical content
- The advantages of integrating D3.js into an AngularJS application
- How to structure and encapsulate a visualization library written in D3.js to use with an AngularJS application

Building a real-time dashboard to visualize server logs

Did you ever wonder how many users visit your web application or how many exceptions your server application raised in the last month? The solution to various similar problems is to simply analyze and visualize the log or access files of the particular application.

In this book, we will develop a real-time dashboard to visualize application logs and the server's system status in the browser. Thus, we will build a custom **Google Analytics**-like visualization dashboard for our own server (see the following figure). Additionally, we want to add custom animation and user interactions—such as selecting data ranges, zooming, and panning—to the visualization.

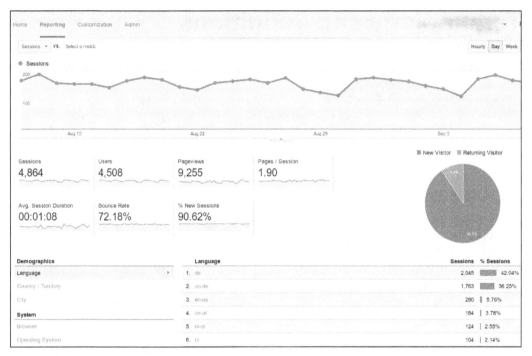

Google Analytics dashboard

The dashboard (frontend) will be capable of loading, parsing, and grouping log files of different formats, filtering data based on selected data ranges and displaying, updating, and animating multiple chart types. We will build the visualization library with D3.js and the application with AngularJS.

While developing this application, we will see all the advantages, problems, and best practices of D3.js and AngularJS in action. Also, you will learn to combine both frameworks to one single application.

During most of the chapters, we will focus on loading log data from static resources. In the last chapter, we will implement a simple web server (backend) using **Node. js** and **Express** to detect log file changes in real time and push these changes to the dashboard using WebSockets and the **Socket.IO** library.

Besides implementing all the functionality, you will also learn how to design and test (we will use unit and integration tests) the frontend components with the test runners, **Karma** and **Protractor**.

Terminology and definitions

Let's start from the beginning. In the following chapters, we will discuss computer graphics and visualizations for the Web. Therefore, it's important to understand the basic terminology of this domain. In this section, I will refresh your knowledge of the two most common image representations (vector and pixel graphics). I will also discuss the web standards that are relevant for graphical applications (DOM, SVG, and so on). If these definitions are not new for you, then nothing can stop you from jumping directly to the next section.

Document Object Model

The **Document Object Model (DOM)** is the tree representation of the hierarchical elements of an HTML document and it was specified by the **World Wide Web Consortium (W3C)**. These elements in the DOM are called *nodes* (for example, html, head, body, and so on), which can have *attributes* (for example, class="header") and *content* (for example, "My Application" is the content of the h1 node). The DOM provides a public JavaScript interface with which we can access nodes and manipulate them.

Let's look at the source code of a simple HTML page to see an example of the DOM tree:

```
<html>
  <head>
    <title>My App</title>
  </head>
  <body>
    <h1 class="header>My Application</h1>
    <p class="content">
      Lorem ipsum dolor sit amet, ...
    </p>
  </body>
</html>
```

Developers often visualize the DOM tree and its hierarchical elements by indenting the HTML code properly. The DOM tree of the previous example can also be displayed and modified with the *developer tools* of a modern browser. See the following screenshot:

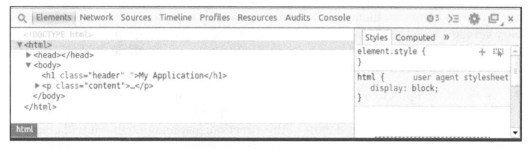

DOM tree in Chrome developer tools

Vector graphics and Scalable Vector Graphics

A **vector graphic** is an image represented solely by the geometric primitives (shape) and attributes (size, margins, appearance, and so on) of its containing elements. These elements can be primitive shapes (such as lines, circles, triangles, and so on) or complex shapes that are composed by these primitives. All elements are included in the graphic; therefore, the whole graphic can be described by implicit mathematical expressions. Thus, the size of a vector graphic is only dependent on the number and complexity of the elements in the image and not on the resolution in which it will be displayed.

Rule of thumb for vector graphics

The more the *elements* in the image, the higher the cost to draw or update the graphic, but in general, the costs do not depend on the resolution of the generated image (lossless rescaling).

Let's look at a simple example. An image of a circle can be fully described by the shape of a circle with the coordinates of its center point and radius. In all modern browsers, we can generate a vector graphic by embedding **Scalable Vector Graphics (SVG)**, a web standard for vector graphics specified by the W3C directly in the DOM, as follows:

```
<html>
  ...
  <body>
    <svg id="vis" width="640" height="480">
```

```
      <circle cx="25" cy="25" r="20" style="fill:red;">
    </svg>
  </body>
</html>
```

All containing elements of a vector graphic are usually stored in a scene graph, a tree representation of the hierarchical elements of the graphic. This concept is very similar to the DOM tree, and in the case of SVG, the scene graph is directly embedded in the DOM tree. We can see this in the previous example (by looking at the svg node) that contains the circle element.

As we mentioned previously, we can also use JavaScript to generate or modify SVGs. Let's use the partially complete helper function that generates and draws SVG nodes. Don't worry about the details of this function; just imagine that it will create a vector graphic element (you can look it up in the source code of this chapter if you are brave enough):

```
<script type="text/javascript">
function VectorGraphic(parent, tag, attrs) {

  var el = document.createElementNS('http://www.w3.org/2000/svg',
  tag);

  ...
  return {
    on: function(event, handler){...},
    fill: function(color){...},
    stroke: function(color){...},
    draw: function() {
      parent.appendChild(el);
    }
  }
}
</script>
```

The preceding function creates a new SVG node and returns a .draw() method. It appends this new element to the parent container. Additionally, it provides methods to style the layout of the new element. Let's use this function to create the same circle from the previous example from within JavaScript:

```
<script type="text/javascript">
  var ctx = document.getElementById('vis');

  var circle = VectorGraphic(ctx, 'circle', {cx:25, cy:25, r:20});

  circle.fill('red');

  circle.draw();
</script>
```

The preceding code will generate the same circle as before with the center point at the coordinates 25, 25 and a radius of 20. The following figure shows the result of the graphic in the browser, where the left-hand side shows the original image and the right-hand side shows the image after zooming in:

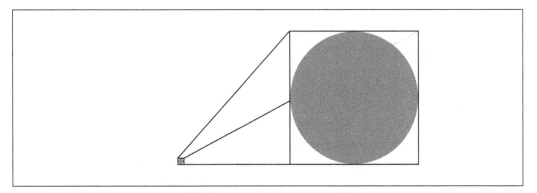

A vector graphic generated in the SVG node (left: normal, right: zoom)

We observe that the circle will always appear in the best resolution no matter how far we zoom into the image. The reason for this is that the vector graphics are recomputed (by the mathematical expressions), redrawn, and rasterized according to the relevant display and zoom factor.

We silently skipped another very important fact of SVGs such that all the elements of the graphic appear in the DOM tree of the SVG node. In our case, we can see in the previous example of the HTML page that the SVG node contains a circle element. This means that the browser also knows about all the elements in the image. Therefore, we can use all built-in capabilities to style and observe these elements. For example, it's possible to attach an event listener with JavaScript to the circle and call event handlers when the user interacts with this element of the graphic. This event handler could look like this:

```
<script type="text/javascript">
  var ctx = document.getElementById('vis');
  var circle = VectorGraphic(ctx, 'circle', {cx:25, cy:25, r:20});
  circle.fill('red');
  circle.on('mouseover', function() {
    this.stroke('blue');
  });
  circle.draw();
</script>
```

Vector graphics (particularly generated with SVG) are used in the Web, in general, to draw graphics that contain a moderate number of elements and when interactions and controls (such as zooming, panning, selecting elements, and so on) are desired. Graphics for high performance with a big number of elements would rather use pixel graphics.

Pixel graphics

A **pixel graphic** (often called as a **raster graphic**) is an image that is represented solely by the pixels in the graphic. Thus, its size is only dependent on the resolution of the image.

Rule of thumb for pixel graphics

The more the *pixels* in the image (the higher the resolution of the image), the higher the cost to draw or update the graphic, but in general, the cost does not depend on the number of elements in the generated image.

In general, pixel graphics are rasterized images of a geometric representation. Therefore, an image of a circle can be just as well defined by the shape of a circle with coordinates of its center point and a radius. The description of the circle is exactly the same as for vector graphics, only the ways of storing and displaying the image are different.

Let's write a partially complete JavaScript helper function to generate pixel graphics with the **Canvas** API. Don't worry about the details of this function; just imagine that it will create a pixel graphic element (you can look it up in the source code of this chapter if you are brave enough):

```
<script type="text/javascript">
function PixelGraphic(parent, tag, attrs) {

  var el = parent.getContext('2d');
  el.beginPath();
  ...
  return {
    stroke: function (color){... },
    fill: function (color){ ... },
    draw: function () {
      el.arc(attrs.cx, attrs.cy, attrs.r, 0, 2*Math.PI);
      ...
    }
  }
}
</script>
```

If we generate such a circle with JavaScript, the resulting code looks very similar to the previous vector graphic example:

```
<script type="text/javascript">
  var ctx = document.getElementById('vis');
  var circle = PixelGraphic(ctx, 'circle', {cx:25, cy:25, r:20});
  circle.fill('red');
  circle.draw();
</script>
```

The preceding code generates a very similar circle element with the center point at the coordinates 25, 25 and a radius of 20. However, if we look at the resulting DOM tree, we observe a small but important difference, that is, the circle element is not visible in the canvas node. Let's look at the HTML code of this example:

```
<html>
  ...
  <body>
    <canvas id="vis" width="640" height="480"></canvas>
  </body>
</html>
```

The pixel graphic in the previous example is now stored in the `canvas` element. As a result, the image is rasterized and transformed to a pixel array of color values. Therefore, the `canvas` element does not contain any information about the elements of the image.

If we look at the result of this code in the browser, we see the exact same image as before with the vector circle. The only small, but very important difference will become visible once we zoom inside the graphic. We will soon start to see pixels instead of a sharp and smooth circle. This effect is visualized in the following figure:

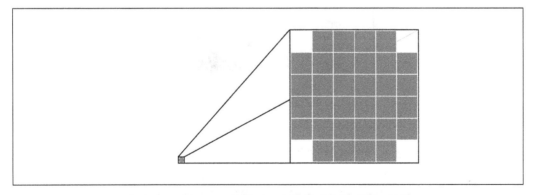

A pixel graphic generated in canvas (left: normal, right: zoom)

This effect can be easily explained if we look closer at how pixel graphics are stored. First, the image is internally drawn on a container with the defined dimension of the image. Then, the image is divided by a raster, which is defined by the image resolution. Finally, the image is stored as pixel values of this raster. If we see a pixelated image, we see exactly these discrete rastered pixel values. The whole process is called **rasterization** and is visualized in the following figure:

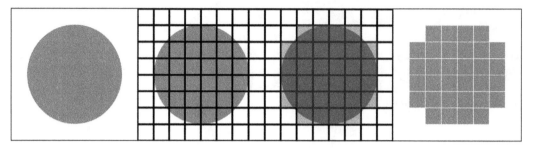

A pixel graphic generated and rasterized in Canvas

Besides lossy rescaling, we can spot another big difference to vector graphics: the browser does not know about the elements in the image. Therefore, it's not possible to see and address the elements of the graphics in the DOM tree anymore. It's not possible anymore to attach an event listener to the circle and call event handlers when the user interacts with an element of the graphic. In pixel graphics, we are primarily interacting with pixel values instead of objects, as we can see in the following figure:

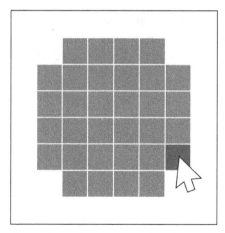

Interaction with the generated pixel graphic

In pixel graphics, we need to think in pixels rather than in elements of an image.

We usually prefer pixel graphics in the browser — particularly generated with Canvas (2D) or WebGL (3D) — for graphics that contain a big number of elements and performance (high frame rate) is more important than the image quality, interactions, and zooming.

Understanding Data-Driven Documents

Data-Driven Documents (D3.js) is a data-driven library for DOM manipulation and a graphical toolkit with maximum compatibility, accessibility, and performance. It utilizes fully the capabilities of modern browsers and web standards (such as HTML, CSS, and SVG).

It is open source and hosted on GitHub (`https://github.com/mbostock/d3`) under a slightly modified BSD 3-clause license; therefore, it can be used in commercial products without being required to release any modifications. By the way, GitHub itself uses D3.js to visualize the contribution history of repositories.

Make yourself familiar with the wiki pages and the API reference on GitHub as they will become your companions during the next weeks:

- Wiki pages (`https://github.com/mbostock/d3/wiki`)
- API reference (`https://github.com/mbostock/d3/wiki/API-Reference`)

Why do we use D3.js?

D3.js is used for various different tasks, but it's mainly used for the following purposes:

- Transforming HTML or SVG elements in the DOM tree, as shown in the following code:

```
<script type="text/javascript">
  // Example for HTML
  // Change the background color of all p elements
  d3.selectAll('p').style('background-color', 'red');
</script>
```

- Transforming data into HTML or SVG elements as follows:

```
<script type="text/javascript">
  // Example for SVG
  d3.selectAll('circle').data(dataArray)
    .enter()
    .append('circle');
</script>
```

- Generating or preparing complex visual content, as shown in the following code:

```
<script type="text/javascript">
  // Create a Chord element
  var chord = d3.layout.chord()
    .sortSubgroups(d3.descending)
    .matrix(matrix);

</script>
```

- Loading data using AJAX requests as follows:

```
<script type="text/javascript">
  // Load external data
  d3.json('data.json', function(error, data){
    // do something with the data
  });
</script>
```

> D3.js is not a chart library! It provides low-level tools to build dynamic visualizations; therefore, many chart libraries are built on top of D3.js.

One reason why D3.js gained a lot of popularity is its *data-driven* approach. Instead of explicitly looping over elements in an array and drawing them on the screen, D3.js allows for an *implicit* declarative representation. In D3.js, we rather think in terms of *how the visualization is composed* than *how each element is arranged in the scene*. The second main reason for its popularity is its *clear focus on its underlying web standards (HTML, SVG, and CSS)*. This brings many advantages such as the following:

- **Compatibility**: D3.js is not abstracting the underlying standards, it's exploiting them. Therefore, developers can use all standard attributes of HTML, SVG, and CSS to compose and style their visualizations rather than learning an abstraction API for the visualization library.

- **Debugging**: D3.js will not only append all HTML elements and styles to the DOM, but it will also append all SVG elements and their CSS attributes. This makes it possible to simply open the developer tools of the browser and look at the generated and modified elements and attributes. It lets developers use their standard debugging tools and workflows that they are already familiar with. Whoever dealt with debugging of pixel graphics libraries (such as OpenGL, WebGL, Canvas, and so on) knows that good debugging capabilities are a real game changer.

- **Performance**: D3.js relies on SVG and therefore facilitates optimizing performance of interactions and animations by giving full access to all SVG features. In most other graphical libraries, one is limited to the capabilities provided by the abstraction layer and the API of the library.

The killer feature – data joins

There is one more feature that distinguishes D3.js from other DOM transforming libraries such as jQuery: the concept of **data joins**. When binding an array of data, D3.js automatically intersects the *old* dataset with the *new* one to generate three new datasets:

- The **enter set** that stores all elements from the *new* dataset that are not in the *old* dataset and therefore need to be added
- The **update set** that stores all elements from the *new* dataset that are already in the *old* dataset and therefore need to be updated
- The **exit set** that stores all the elements from the *old* dataset that are not in the *new* dataset and therefore need to be removed

The following figure visualizes this intersection, where the *old* dataset is called **Selection** and the *new* dataset is called **Data**:

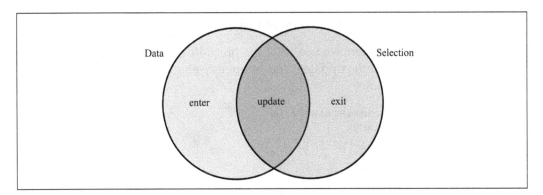

Data joins in D3.js

This technique is often referred to as **data binding** because we are literally binding an array of elements to a Selection of elements. However, now we know that data joins are not just data bindings, but they additionally intersect the datasets.

Let's look at a simple example. In general, the data-driven approach of D3.js allows developers to declare the manipulations of HTML or SVG elements based on CSS selectors. This is very similar to jQuery; therefore, I will also show the corresponding code using jQuery:

```
<script type="text/javascript">
  // with jQuery
  $('p').css('background-color', 'red');
  // with D3.js
  d3.selectAll('p').style('background-color', 'red');
</script>
```

However, the big difference is that D3.js implements data joins, which gives developers the access to match an array of elements (the *new* dataset) to a Selection (the *old* dataset). Corresponding with the **enter**, **update**, and **exit** sets from the previous intersection figure, D3.js can return these intersected datasets using the following functions:

- `selection.data(dataSet).enter()` for elements that are new to the dataset and not yet in the current Selection

- `selection.data(dataSet)` for elements that are already existent in the dataset

- `selection.data(dataSet).exit()` for elements that are removed from the dataset and still existent in the current Selection

Let's look at an example where we use all of the preceding methods. First, we will write a function that appends, updates, and removes p elements in the DOM. Then, we will play around with it:

```
<script type="text/javascript">
function join_p(dataSet) {
  var el = d3.select('body');

  var join = el
    // get the selection of all p elements
    .selectAll('p')
    // join the selection with the dataset
    .data(dataSet);

  // elements not yet in the selection
  // they need to be added
  join.enter().append('p');

  // elements currently in the selection
  // they need to be updated
```

```
        join.text(function(d) { return d; });

        // elements still in selection
        // they need to be removed
        join.exit().remove('p');}
    </script>
```

Let's play with this function in the developer tools of the browser. At first, we see a blank page without any p elements in the DOM. Okay, now we call the `join_p(['append', 'to', 'DOM'])` function from the console inside the browser.

We observe that three paragraphs appear with the content append, to, and DOM; we can also look at the DOM tree in the developer tools:

```
<body>
    <p>append</p><p>to</p><p>DOM</p>
</body>
```

So what happened here? In the `join_p()` function, we first created a Selection of all p elements in the body using `.selectAll('p')` and then created a data join with the `['append', 'to', 'DOM']` dataset using `.data(dataSet)`. It seems weird that we call `.selectAll('p')` where not a single p element exists yet in the DOM. However, if we think in terms of data joins, we solely create an empty Selection of p elements. This makes sense immediately after calling the enter function, which returns all elements that are not yet existing in this Selection. In our case of the empty Selection, this function returns all the elements of the dataset. Finally, we just need to append them to the DOM using the `.append('p')` function.

In the following line, the `join` variable returns all elements of the current Selection and we just appended three new elements to it. The `.text()` method updates all elements of the current Selection and sets the value of the array element as text of the corresponding p tag (this method is called dynamic properties and will be explained in more detail in the following chapter). The last method, `.exit()`, returns no elements because all elements are available in the dataset and in the Selection. The following figure shows how the Selection changes with the dataset:

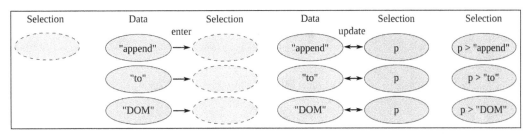

Adding elements to a Selection and updating them

If we now call the `join_p()` function again, this time with the following dataset `join_p(['modify', 'in', 'DOM'])`, we see that the text of the first two paragraphs will change as follows:

```
<body>
  <p>modify</p><p>in</p><p>DOM</p>
</body>
```

Despite the previous function call, the Selection of p elements now is not empty, but contains the three previous elements. This means that both `.enter()` and `.exit()` methods will return no elements. The `join` variable solely contains the new updated elements whose paragraph text is correspondingly updated. We can see the effect on the Selection in the following figure:

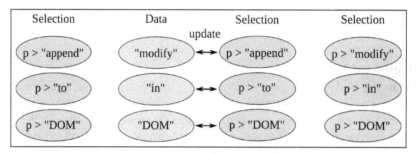

Updating elements of a Selection

Finally, we can try to call `join_p([])` with an empty dataset. As we could imagine by now, this results in all paragraphs being removed. The `.exit()` function will return all elements of the Selection because the dataset contains no elements. Calling `.remove()` on these elements will remove them from the DOM. We can observe the change of the Selection in the following figure:

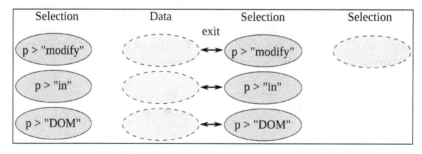

Removing elements from a Selection

 Data joins are data bindings with access to the intersection of the dataset and the Selection.

The concept of data joins enable the developer to append new data to a graphic when new data is available, to update existing data and to remove data from the graphic when it is not available anymore. Instead of redrawing the complete image, the elements of the graphic are transformed.

Finding resources

Michael Bostock provides an extensive source of detailed information on D3.js, helpful posts, and lots of examples. Once you are stuck or need to find particular information on specific topics or examples, I recommend you to read through the following links:

- Michael Bostock's web page at `http://bost.ocks.org/mike/`
- Infinite amount of examples and demos at `http://bl.ocks.org/mbostock`
- Stack Overflow questions at `http://stackoverflow.com/questions/tagged/d3.js`

If you Google D3.js, you will find a lot of additional resources; however, most of them are just dealing with the basics. To get a good and deeper understanding of D3.js, I would rather advise you to look up the relevant chapters in the book *Mastering D3.js, Pablo Navarro Castillo, Packt Publishing*, or look directly into the source code of D3.js on GitHub.

D3.js meets AngularJS

AngularJS is a JavaScript framework that modernizes development of web applications in multiple ways; it introduces client-side templates, MVC/MVVM pattern, scoping, two-way data binding, dependency injection, and so on. Therefore, it's our JavaScript application framework of choice. At this point, I assume that you are already familiar with the main concepts of AngularJS and you know when and how to apply them. If there are still problems, I would recommend you to read the relevant chapters in the book *Mastering Web Application Development with AngularJS* by Pawel Kozlowski and Peter Bacon Darwin, published by Packt Publishing.

Theoretically, we can simply add a D3.js visualization library to the same application that also uses AngularJS without caring about modules, isolation, dependency injection, and so on without any extra effort.

However, once we know how awesome AngularJS is, we want to fully exploit every single advantage of this framework. Having said that, we want every component of the application being injectable, maintainable, and testable. We want to extend HTML syntax and add custom directives to templates. We want proper scope isolation. We want to put common tasks into reusable services. We want to use dependency injection on every single component of the application. We want to integrate D3.js into an application *the Angular way*.

Testable and maintainable components

AngularJS strongly focuses on testability and maintainability of the components of an application. Once we use plain D3.js to modify the DOM in order to load data and create graphical content, it will become very complex and uncomfortable to test single components or the whole application. We will use the full power of AngularJS, the concepts of dependency injection, modularization, isolation, and directives to create testable components.

Custom directives

AngularJS lets you develop your own **directives** that extend the HTML syntax to create reusable components for HTML. This is exactly what we want: a reusable component for each different type of visualization that we are going to build. We aim to declare the different elements of a visualization like in the following example:

```html
<html>
  <head>
    <script>
    ...
    app.directive('d3Map', function(){ ... });
    app.directive('d3LineChart', function(){ ... });
    app.directive('d3ScatterPlot', function(){ ... });
    app.directive('d3ChordDiagram', function(){ ... });
    </script>
  </head>
  <body>
    <d3-map></d3-map>

    <d3-line-chart data="data"></d3-line-chart>
    <d3-scatter-plot data="data"></d3-scatter-plot>
    <d3-chord-diagram data="data"></d3-chord-diagram>
  </body>
</html>
```

We can immediately see that this is a very clean and elegant way to embed your visualization components in the HTML document.

Custom filters

AngularJS introduces **filters** in frontend templates that allow you to modify variables and filter arrays directly inside the template. For our visualization component, we want to create custom filters (for example, to clamp the dataset to a specific range) that can be applied to all graphics at once. Additionally, we want these filters to be autoupdated whenever data is selected in one graphic as follows:

```html
<html>
  <head>
    <script>
    ...
    app.filter('startDate', function(){ ... });
    </script>
  </head>
  <body>
    <d3-line-chart data="timeData | startDate:'01.01.2015'"></d3-
    line-chart>
    <d3-scatter-plot data="timeData | startDate:
    '01.01.2015'"></d3-scatter-plot>
  </body>
</html>
```

Custom loading and parsing service

AngularJS emphasizes the concepts of **services** to implement common functionalities. We want to implement a data loading and parsing service that uses AngularJS' **Promises** and the capabilities of D3.js parsing functions at the same time. The service should be used like this:

```html
<script type="text/javascript">
  app.controller('MainCtrl', ['$scope', 'myService',

    function($scope, myService) {
      myService.get('data.json').then(function(data){
        scope.data = data;
      });
    }
  }]);
</script>
```

A brief overview of visualization tools for the Web

Now, let me explain why we are using D3.js and not any other similar visualization library to manipulate vector graphics.

When I started with web development in 2004, vector graphics and interactive applications were mostly embedded as Flash objects into web pages. The main reason for this was the lack of web standards for vector graphics or good and powerful JavaScript libraries for image manipulation. It was difficult to create interactive visualizations that integrate into the underlying page because functionalities (such as layouts and fonts) defined in CSS and user interactions written in JavaScript were not available in embedded objects. Thus, these visualization objects often felt like a strange add-on to the underlying application, where fonts, size, and colors were not completely matching with the application. A typical code example for an embedded visualization looks like this:

```
<html>
  ...
  <body>
  <object id="vis" width="50" height="30">
    <param name="movie" value="vis.swf">
    <embed src="vis.swf" type="application/x-shockwave-flash">
  </object>
  </body>
</html>
```

We can see in the preceding example that the compiled and embedded `vis.swf` Flash object is completely isolated from the scope of the host application. In addition to the web browser, we would also need a plugin that can interpret the Flash binary object. While the application and the embedded visualization have the same task—displaying data on a web page—they are not sharing common styles or a common scope for user interactions.

Java and Flash

One of the first consistent toolsets for interactive data visualization for the Web was the Java library Prefuse, which was published by Jeffrey Heer in 2007, who, at this time, is a member at the Berkley Visualization Lab. Prefuse provided rich tools for data modeling and interactive graphics. The visualization could be embedded as Java applets into a web page, but this required the Java runtime environment to be installed on every browser that wants to display the visualization.

Later in 2008, Heer released the first version of Flare, a port of the Prefuse library to ActionScript, which could compile the visualization to a more common Flash object. A simple application that shows three circles with different *x* coordinates in an image with the size of 50 x 30 pixel looks like this with Flare:

```
[SWF(width="50", height="30")]
public class Vis extends Sprite
{
  public function Vis()
  {
    // Define the dataset
    var data:Array = [15, 25, 35];
    for each (var d:int in data) {
      var sprite:Sprite = new Sprite();
      // Draw and color the circles
      sprite.graphics.beginFill(0xff0000, 1.0);
      sprite.graphics.drawCircle(0, 0, 5);
      this.addChild(sprite);
      // Set the coordinates of the circle
      sprite.x = d;
      sprite.y = 15;
    }
  }
}
```

Looking at the preceding code, we can see that in each loop, we create a drawing container (sprite) and a circle element. We also color it and with `sprite.x = d`, we set the *x* coordinate of the `sprite` container to the current value `d` of the `data` array. Don't worry if this code looks quite complicated to you because this is exactly the reason why I am showing it. It's complicated and not intuitive to create containers, add elements, and move containers to the position where we want to display the circle. Furthermore, to run this example in the browser, we have a very similar problem as before with Prefuse: each browser needs the Flash runtime installed. The resulting image generated by the previous code will look like the following figure:

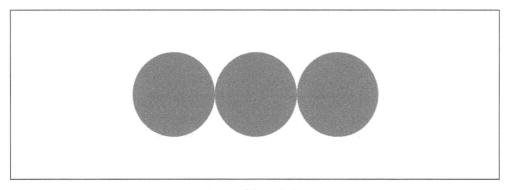

Image of three circles

Raphaël (JavaScript – SVG/VML)

By 2008, most of the major browsers provided native support for SVG and signified the certain end of Flash in the upcoming years. However, Internet Explorer implemented a different markup language for vector graphics than SVG; it used the similar, but different **Vector Markup Language (VML)**.

In 2009, Dmitry Baranovskiy announced the first release of Raphaël, a JavaScript library that aims to simplify the manipulation of vector graphics by providing a JavaScript API for SVG with a compatibility layer for VML for Internet Explorer. The representation of graphics inside the DOM not only enabled the use of JavaScript event handlers for user interactions on elements of the image, but it also enabled the use of CSS to style these elements. This was a huge step towards open web standards, accessibility, and acceptance of SVG. An example of drawing the same three circles looks like this:

```
<script type="text/javascript">
  // Define the dataset
  var data = [15, 25, 35];
  // Draw the canvas
  var paper = Raphael(0, 0, 50, 30);
  // Draw and color the circles
  for (var i = 0; i < 3; i ++) {
    var circle = paper.circle(data[i], 15, 5);
    circle.attr('fill', 'red');
  }
</script>
```

Again, we generate a circle with the *x* coordinate of the data array each time we loop over the array. In a modern browser, the preceding code produces an SVG image that looks exactly like the previous example, but additionally outputs directly to the DOM of the HTML page. It adds three circle elements with different *x* coordinates of the center point to the DOM tree inside the SVG node. The generated SVG code embedded in the web page will look like this:

```
<html>
  ...
  <body>
    <svg width="50" height="30">
      <circle cx="15" cy="15" r="5" style="fill:red;">
      <circle cx="25" cy="15" r="5" style="fill:red;">
      <circle cx="35" cy="15" r="5" style="fill:red;">
    </svg>
  </body>
</html>
```

Protovis (JavaScript – SVG)

In the same year at Stanford, Michael Bostock and Jeffrey Heer published the visualization library Protovis for SVG manipulation in JavaScript. Its new data-driven approach allowed the developers to declare the representation of data, rather than looping and drawing multiple elements explicitly. The following code uses Protovis to generate the exact same SVG graphic of the three circles shown in the previous figure:

```
<script type="text/javascript">
  // Define the dataset
  var data = [15, 25, 35];
  // Define the canvas
  var vis = new pv.Panel()
    .width(50)
    .height(30);
  // Define the circles and their color
  vis.add(pv.Dot)
    .data(data)
    .left(function(d) { return d; })
    .bottom(15)
    .radius(5)
    .fillStyle('red');
  // Draw the canvas and the circles
  vis.render();
</script>
```

The main difference in the previous example is that the explicit loop over the data array in Raphaël is replaced by the a implicit data() function in Protovis, where the *x* coordinate of each circle is called as a function that returns the current element of the data array.

D3.js (JavaScript – HTML/SVG)

In 2011, when SVG was finally supported in all major browsers and Internet Explorer, the same authors of Protovis—Michael Bostock and further members of the Stanford Visualization Group—published D3.js, a more generalized version of Protovis with built-in support for animations. The goal was not to restrict the library anymore on just the SVG object, but to access the complete DOM tree and use all of its features and underlying standards. Therefore, all updates and extensions for HTML and CSS (for example, new attributes, and so on) are immediately available in D3.js. To support dynamic visualizations, D3.js also introduced the concepts of data joins, which let the developer add, update, and remove elements depending on data that was added, updated, or removed from a Selection (this will be discussed in more detail in the next chapter).

The same graphic as previously generated with Raphael and Protovis can be created with D3.js as follows:

```
<script type="text/javascript">
   // Define the dataset
   var data = [15, 25, 35];
   // Draw the canvas
   var vis = d3.select('body')
      .append('svg')
      .attr('width', 50)
      .attr('height', 30);
   // Draw and color the circles
   vis.selectAll('circle')
      .data(data)
      .enter().append('circle')
      .attr('cx', function(d) { return d; })
      .attr('cy', 15)
      .attr('r', 5)
      .style('fill', 'red');
</script>
```

We remark that D3.js implements more general methods, for example, attr('r') that uses the underlying SVG attribute r for the radius explicitly instead of the radius() function, which is an abstraction of the SVG attribute r in Protovis.

The selectAll().data().enter() construct in this static example looks more complicated than the simple data() function of Protovis, but it implements data joins to create new elements for new data in the Selection. Therefore, it will be very useful to update dynamic graphics in the following chapters of this book.

 D3.js forces developers to use the underlying standards HTML, CSS, and SVG instead of providing an abstraction of these attributes.

Canvas API (JavaScript – Canvas)

Since the introduction of HTML5, we can also use the Canvas element and its JavaScript API to draw the exact same circles as in the previous examples. The performance of Canvas is much better than SVG when drawing large amount of objects/elements. However, the content of the Canvas will be drawn as a pixel graphic and no element will be appended to the DOM or the Canvas node, which is a huge drawback.

Three.js (JavaScript – WebGL)

With WebGL that was introduced in 2011, we can also draw the example of the three circles using the *Three.js* JavaScript library. WebGL has access to hardware acceleration of the operating system and is mainly used for 3D graphics. The resulting image is a pixel graphic. However, it's worth mentioning that it's not available in all modern browsers.

Summary

In this chapter, we discovered the benefits of the powerful combination of SVG, D3.js, and AngularJS. SVG are lossless and rescalable *vector graphics* that are supported in all modern browsers. All the elements of an image are directly appended to the DOM tree of the HTML page, which makes debugging with the browser's *developer tools* very comfortable. D3.js is a versatile low-level library for generating interactive graphical content based on the underlying standards (HTML, CSS, and SVG).

In the first section of this chapter, we outlined the sample application that we will develop during this book: a dashboard for interactive real-time visualizations of web server logs and system status.

You learned about the concept of *data joins*, which differentiates D3.js from other DOM-transformation libraries like jQuery. Developers can not only bind data to a Selection, but also retrieve the enter, update, and exit sets (the intersection of the dataset with a current Selection of DOM elements).

D3.js and AngularJS can live side by side in an application, but we want to integrate the D3.js visualization into the AngularJS application *the Angular way*. This enhances maintainability, testability, and reusability of all components of an application.

In the next chapter, we will start to develop our first visualization with D3.js. In the first step, you will learn about *Selections* and *transformations* and use them to draw circles in SVG. Then, we will apply the concepts of *data binding* and *data joins* to draw a simple scatter chart based on an array of data samples.

2
Getting Started with D3.js

In this chapter, we will build our first simple scatter plot application using D3.js. Don't worry if you have no experience with D3.js, we will cover all the necessary topics from setting up a simple HTML template, selecting DOM elements, and binding data to DOM elements.

First, you will learn how to draw vector graphics with the use of D3.js. To get started, we will set up a simple D3.js application template that serves for all examples in this chapter.

In the second section, you will learn how to select and modify elements from the DOM and change their attributes and their appearance. Starting with modifying HTML elements, I will answer some common questions to understand the similarities and differences between D3.js and other JavaScript libraries. We will then apply these transformations to SVG elements.

Then, we will take a closer look at D3 Selections and CSS Selectors in D3.js. This will help us to understand how to find and select specific elements in the DOM and how these elements are stored in the Selection.

In the next section, we will look at data binding and introduce dynamic properties, an important characteristic of data-driven libraries. We will continue to discuss data joins and the update pattern in D3.js, which helps us to modify elements based on the difference of a Selection and the bound data. At the end of this chapter, we will use all of this knowledge to draw a simple scatter chart with D3.js based on an array of data.

In this chapter, you will learn the following topics:

- Including D3.js in our applications
- Selecting and modifying HTML and SVG elements
- Applying selectors to find elements in the DOM
- Storing elements in a Selection

- Binding data to elements
- Using dynamic properties
- Drawing a simple scatter chart

Building a simple scatter plot application

Did you ever wonder how Google Analytics, GitHub, or Wolfram Alpha create these beautiful and colorful plots of your data? Did you know that with D3.js, you have the power to create similar or even better visualizations right at your fingertips?

In this chapter, we will build a simple scatter plot application. This type of plot can be used to visualize the areas and frequency of clicks on a web page; the following figure shows an example of such a plot. The circles indicate typical areas of the website that are often clicked on, whereas the size and color of the circles show the amount of clicks on an area. To keep things simple, in the beginning, we will create a scatter plot and fill it with random data.

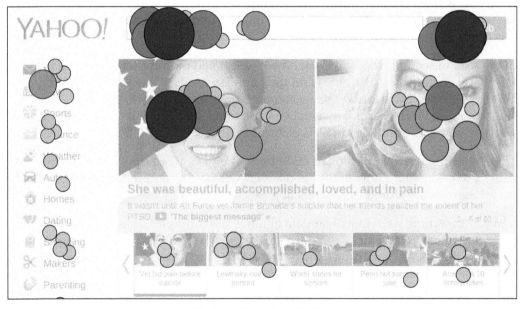

Simple scatter plot application

Creating an HTML template for D3.js

To set up a template page for all visualization examples, we first need to download D3.js and include it to the application. In this book, we will use version 3.5.5, but all of the examples should also work with slightly different versions (~3.4.12 and ~3.5.0). There are multiple ways to add D3.js to an application:

- Installing it with the package manager bower (recommended):

  bower install d3#3.5.5

- Loading it from a **Content Delivery Network (CDN)** (`//cdnjs.cloudflare.com/ajax/libs/d3/3.5.5/d3.js`).

- Downloading it and storing it to a `libs` directory (`https://github.com/mbostock/d3/releases/tag/v3.5.5`).

The easiest way to use D3.js in our application is to simply download D3.js directly from GitHub and extract it into the `libs` directory. In contrast to the CDN method, this does not require an active Internet connection while developing. However, the recommended way is to use a package manager such as bower to manage and configure all third-party dependencies.

So, go ahead and download D3.js from GitHub, extract it, and store the `d3.js` file in the `libs` directory! Now, we can create an `index.html` file and reference D3.js as a JavaScript library in the header as follows:

```
<!DOCTYPE html>
<html>
  <head>
    <script src="libs/d3.js" charset="UTF-8"></script>
  </head>
  <body>
    <!-- D3.js example go here  -->
  </body>
</html>
```

Bear in mind that due to the usage of Greek letters in the unminified version of D3.js, we also need to set the `charset` attribute of the `<script>` tag to `UTF-8`. In the whole book, I will use the exact same HTML template as used in the preceding code for all code samples; I will solely change the body of the HTML page. Whenever we modify the `<head>` tag to add more libraries, I will indicate this in the relevant examples.

Selecting and modifying DOM elements

D3.js provides a variety of functions to manipulate elements of the DOM tree, such as setting their attributes, changing their content, creating new elements, or removing them. As you learned in the first chapter, instead of looping through elements and modifying them one by one, with D3.js, we are applying transformations in a declarative way directly to an array of elements. We call the object that stores all the elements in an array a **Selection**.

To extract such an array of elements from the DOM tree, D3.js offers the `d3.selectAll(selector)` function to select all elements of a specific type and the `d3.select(selector)` function to select just a single element. While both functions return a Selection that contains an array of elements, the latter function returns an array with solely a single element.

To tell D3.js which elements we want to select, we use so-called CSS selectors (these are the standard CSS selectors that most developers are already familiar with). Thus, a selector is usually a tag name (`body`, `div`, and so on), an ID (`#head`, `#content`, and so on), or a class name (`.nav-item`, `.media`, and so on). We will take a closer look at selectors in a later section of this chapter.

Once we have a Selection, we can apply transformations to all containing elements. For example, we can modify their HTML attributes with the `.attr()` method, we can set CSS styles with the `.style()` method, or remove elements from the DOM with the `.remove()` method. We will see more transformations in the next section; for now, let's just try all of this and look at some code:

```html
<p>Some fruits:</p>
<p class="item" id="first-item">Apple</p>
<p class="item" id="second-item">Banana</p>
<p class="item" id="third-item">Orange</p>

<script type="text/javascript">
  // Select all p tags
  var ps = d3.selectAll('p');
  // Select all elements with the class 'item'
  var items = d3.selectAll('.item');
  // Select the first element with the id 'first-item'
  var first = d3.select('#first-item');

  // Add a HTML attribute to all p tags
  ps.attr('align', 'center');
  // Change the background-color of the items
  items.style('background-color', 'red');
  // Remove the element #first-item from the DOM
  first.remove();
</script>
```

In the following screenshot, we can see the resulting HTML page before transformation on the HTML elements:

Some fruits:

Apple

Banana

Orange

HTML page before previous transformations

The following image shows the HTML page after transformation:

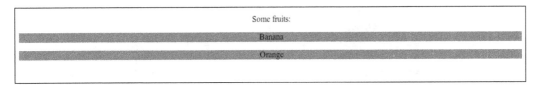

HTML page after previous transformations

When looking at this simple example, the preceding code may look very familiar as it can be written in a very similar way with plain JavaScript or the jQuery library. In general, some people come up with concrete questions when seeing an example like this, so I want to go ahead and answer them:

- **This example looks pretty boring. Why is it useful?**: It is useful because it shows how to use D3.js to select elements from the DOM and to transform all the elements of the Selection in a data-driven way, for example, we write `items.style('background-color', 'red');` to modify all elements with an `item` class.

- **I can do the exact same thing with other libraries. Where exactly is the difference?**: Despite other libraries, `d3.selectAll()` returns a D3-Selection — an object that stores and groups all the selected elements and offers specific methods that are different from other libraries. I will just name a few of these functions that are specific for D3.js: the `.data()` method for data binding and dynamic properties, the `.enter()` and `.exit()` methods for data joins — we will see both these methods later in this chapter — and the `.transition()` method for animations that will be discussed in a later chapter.

- **This example is not at all related with computer graphics or generating visualizations. Why do I need all of these?**: We need all of these because in the previous example, we selected and modified HTML elements in the DOM tree. In the first chapter of this book, you learned about **Scalable Vector Graphics (SVG)** and that the scene graph of SVG—the container that stores all the elements of the image—is directly embedded into the DOM tree. This means that we can also use D3.js to select, style, and modify all the graphical elements of a SVG.

Now, we will try a similar example where we apply transformations to the SVG elements:

```
<svg width="400" height="120">
  <text x="10" y="40">Some shapes:</text>
  <rect class="item" id="first-item" width="100" height="50" x="0"
    y="50" />
  <circle class="item" id="second-item" cx="150" cy="25" r="25" />
  <line class="item" id="third-item" x2="400" y2="100"
    style="stroke:black" />
</svg>

<script type="text/javascript">
  // Select all circle tags
  var circ = d3.selectAll('circle');
  // Select all elements with the class 'item'
  var items = d3.selectAll('.item');
  // Select the first element with the id 'first-item'
  var first = d3.select('#first-item');

  // Add a SVG attribute to all circle tags
  circ.attr('r', '50');
  // Change the fill color of the items
  items.style('fill', 'red');
  // Remove the element #first-item from the DOM
  first.remove();
</script>
```

In the following figure, we can see the HTML page from the previous transformations on the SVG elements:

HTML page before previous transformations

The following image shows the HTML page after transformation:

HTML page after previous transformations

We observed that we can apply the transformations to the SVG elements in the DOM tree that allows you to modify the graphical content. In the example, we used very basic transformations that can also be written in the SVG itself or by including CSS styles. In the *Binding data to DOM elements* section, you will learn more advanced techniques on how to create and modify the graphical content completely with D3.js.

A closer look at Selections

A **Selection** is a subclass of the array object that stores grouped arrays of DOM elements and implements methods to modify all of its elements.

Let's look at an example with the most basic Selection:

```
<svg width="400" height="200">
  <circle cx="50" cy="50" r="40" />
  <circle cx="150" cy="50" r="40" />
</svg>

<script type="text/javascript">
  // Get a Selection of the circles
  var circles = d3.selectAll('circle');

  console.log(circles);
  // [[<circle />, <circle />]]
</script>
```

The Selection of the preceding example contains an outer array with one element inside. This inner element is an array that contains two DOM elements — the two circles. Whenever a Selection is applied via d3.selectAll(), it will return just a single outer group with an array of resulting elements inside. Whenever Selections are nested — .selectAll() is called on another Selection — D3.js will group the result; we see this in the following example.

```
<svg width="400" height="200">
  <g>
    <circle cx="50" cy="50" r="40" />
    <circle cx="150" cy="50" r="40" />
```

```
    </g>
    <g>
      <circle cx="250" cy="50" r="40" />
      <circle cx="350" cy="50" r="40" />
    </g>
</svg>

<script type="text/javascript">
  // Get a Selection of the groups
  var groups = d3.selectAll('g');

  // Get a nested Selection of the circles
  var circles = groups.selectAll('circle');

  console.log(circles);
  // [[<circle />, <circle />], [<circle />, <circle />]]
</script>
```

D3.js provides a variety of functions that can be applied to Selections; I will list the most important ones:

- Selections:
  - .select(selector|node)
  - .selectAll(selector|nodes)
  - .filter(selector)
  - .sort(comparator)

- Content modification:
  - .attr(name[, value])
  - .style(name[, value[, priority]])
  - .property(name[, value])
  - .text([value])
  - .append(name)
  - .insert(name[, before])
  - .remove()

- Data binding:
  - .data([values[, key]])
  - .enter()
  - .exit()

- Animation and interaction:
  - ○ `.on(type[, listener[, capture]])`
  - ○ `.transition()`
- Flow control:
  - ○ `.each(function)`
  - ○ `.call(function[, arguments...])`

In this chapter, we will mostly use the methods for content modification, so you will spot many of them in the examples. Therefore, I will briefly discuss them in this section. Selectors and Selection functions as well as flow control functions are explained in the next section. The data binding methods will be discussed in a later section of this chapter and animation and interaction will appear in more detail later in this book.

Refer to the D3.js API available at `https://github.com/mbostock/d3/wiki/Selections` for detailed information on all these functions.

selection.attr(name[, value])

This sets the attribute of a DOM element if the value is defined; otherwise, it returns the current value of the attribute:

```
<p>Apple, Banana and Orange</p>

<script type="text/javascript">
  // Set the attribute
  d3.select('p').attr('class', 'my-class');
  // Get the attribute
  console.log(d3.select('p').attr('class'));
  // 'my-class'
</script>
```

selection.style(name[, value[, priority]])

This sets the CSS style of a DOM element if the value is defined; otherwise, it returns the current value of the CSS style. This function also accepts an object literal to set multiple CSS styles at once. The priority for the CSS style can take either the value `null` or `important`:

```
<p>Apple, Banana and Orange</p>

<script type="text/javascript">
  // Set the CSS style
```

```
    d3.select('p').style('color', 'red');
    d3.select('p').style({'font-size': 14, 'font-weigth': 'bold'});
    // Get the CSS style
    console.log(d3.select('p').style('color'));
    // 'rgb(255, 0, 0)'
</script>
```

selection.property(name[, value])

This sets the property of a DOM element if the value is defined; otherwise, it returns the current value of the property. This function also accepts an object literal to set multiple properties at once. These HTML properties are usually not assignable by standard attributes or styles, such as `checked`, `selected`, and so on:

```
<input type="checkbox" name="my-box" >

<script type="text/javascript">
    // Set the property
    d3.select('input').property('checked', true);
    // Get the property
    console.log(d3.select('input').property('checked'));
    // true
</script>
```

selection.text([value])

This sets the text content (based on the `textContent` property) of a DOM element if the value is defined; otherwise, it returns the current text content of the element. This function will override all existing child elements of the element:

```
<p>Apple, Banana and Orange</p>

<script type="text/javascript">
    // Set the text content
    d3.select('p').text('I prefer meat.');
    // Get the text content
    console.log(d3.select('p').text());
    // 'I prefer meat.'
</script>
```

selection.append(name)

This appends a `name` element as the last child to the current Selection as follows:

```
<p>Apple, Banana and Orange</p>

<script type="text/javascript">
  // Append a p element
  d3.select('p')
    .append('p').text('I also eat meat.');
</script>
```

The preceding code will insert the second p element after the original one, as shown in the following code:

```
<p>Apple, Banana and Orange</p>
<p>I also eat meat.</p>
```

selection.insert(name[, before])

This inserts a `name` element before the first matching element with the `before` selector of the current Selection:

```
<p class="first">Apple, Banana and Orange</p>
<p class="second">Kiwi, Grapes and Pineapple</p>

<script type="text/javascript">
  // Insert a p element
  d3.select('body')
    .insert('p', '.first').text('I like fruits.');
</script>
```

The preceding code will insert the new p element before the first one as follows:

```
<p>I like fruits.</p>
<p class="first">Apple, Banana and Orange</p>
<p class="second">Kiwi, Grapes and Pineapple</p>
```

selection.remove()

This removes all elements of the current Selection from the DOM:

```
<p>I like fruits.</p>
<p class="second">Apple, Banana and Orange</p>

<script type="text/javascript">
  // Remove the element with class  second
  d3.select('.second').remove();
</script>
```

The preceding code will remove the second element from the DOM as follows:

```
<p>I like fruits.</p>
```

Finding elements in the DOM with Selectors

At the beginning of this chapter, we saw that D3.js uses CSS Selectors to select elements in the DOM tree with the d3.select(selector) function and the d3.selectAll(selector) function. This means that in general, we can use selectors by the tag name: body, div, the ID: #head, #content, the class name: .nav-item, .media, and attributes: [width=100], [align=center].

To find the desired elements, selectors can also be applied hierarchically to elements inside elements by containment: svg circle (circle tags in svg tags), div p (p tags in div tags), and by ancestors: svg > circle (circle tags with a parent svg tag), div > p (p tags with a parent div tag).

Also, they can be logically combined by logical and: .item[width=100] (selects .item AND [width=100]), .this.that (selects .this AND .that) and logical or: .item, [width=100] (selects .item OR [width=100]), .this, .that (selects .this OR .that).

 A well-arranged list of all available CSS selectors is provided on the W3schools website (http://www.w3schools.com/cssref/css_selectors.asp).

While working with D3.js, you will most probably use the common CSS 1 and CSS 2 selectors. For more advanced Selections, you can also use the CSS 3 selectors; however, they are not supported in all browsers.

In particular, D3.js uses the native CSS selector implementation of the browser. This means that the CSS 1 and CSS 2 selectors are fully available across all common browsers, whereas CSS 3 selectors are solely available in modern browsers. To ensure full backwards compatibility for complex selectors, we can simply include the JavaScript selector engine Sizzle (http://sizzlejs.com/) to the application. D3.js will automatically use Sizzle if it's already loaded. A typical setup would look like this:

```
<html>
  <head>
    <script src="libs/sizzle.js"></script>
    <script src="libs/d3.js" charset="UTF-
      8"></script>

  </head>
  ...
</html>
```

d3.select(selector)

This selects an array of elements that matches the CSS Selector and returns a Selection of a single element:

```
<p>I like fruits.</p>
<p>Apple, Banana and Orange</p>

<script type="text/javascript">
  // Select the first element
  var elem = d3.select('p:first-child');
</script>
```

d3.select(node)

Another way to get a Selection of an element is to use d3.select(node) or d3.selectAll(nodes) on the DOM elements itself. This is useful when we already have the DOM element and want to make a D3-Selection out of this element. This enables us to use all the methods of the D3-Selection on this element, thus transforming a DOM element—that might be selected by plain JavaScript or another library—to a D3-Selection. Let's see an example:

```
<form></form>

<script type="text/javascript">
  // document is the global root DOM element
  console.log(document);
  // #document
  // doc is now a Selection
  var doc = d3.select(document);

  // Get a DOM Element
  var dom_elem = document.getElementsByTagName('form')[0];
  // elem is now a Selection
  var elem = d3.select(dom_elem);
</script>
```

We will also use this in the setter functions of dynamic properties to transform the this keyword—that references the current DOM element—into a Selection. We will see this applied in the next section; here is an example of how we create the Selection:

```
    // we are in a scope, where the keyword
    // this references a DOM element p
    console.log(this);
    // <p class="item" id="first-item">Apple</p>
  // self is now a Selection containing this element
var self = d3.select(this);
```

The flow control functions of Selections are useful helpers to apply functions to all elements of a Selection. I will give a brief description of these functions now because we will often need to select the current DOM node via d3.select(this).

selection.each(function)

The .each() method calls the function argument for each element inside the Selection, as shown in the following code:

```
<p>I like fruits.</p>
<p>Apple, Banana and Orange</p>

<script type="text/javascript">
  // Invokes the function for each element
  d3.selectAll('p').each(function(d, i){
    var self = d3.select(this);
    // Output the text of every element
    console.log(self.text());
  });
</script>
```

The preceding code will output the text of both p elements.

selection.call(function[, arguments…])

The .call() method is very similar to the native Function.prototype.call function. It invokes the function once and passes the current selection Selection as the first argument and other optional user-defined arguments to this function:

```
<p>I like fruits.</p>
<p>Apple, Banana and Orange</p>

<script type="text/javascript">
  function set_custom_attr(selection, attr, value) {
    selection
      .attr(attr, value);
  }

  // Invokes the function once
  d3.selectAll('p').call(set_custom_attr, 'align', 'center');
</script>
```

In this simple example, we solely change the `align` attribute on the `p` elements:

```
<p align="center">I like fruits.</p>
<p align="center">Apple, Banana and Orange</p>
```

Binding data to DOM elements

Data binding techniques are very powerful in D3.js because they enable us to generate graphical content based on data. In general, with the data-driven approach, we can declare the graphical elements to match the data instead of looping through the data and drawing the elements one by one.

selection.data(values[, key])

D3-Selections provide the `.data([values[, key]])` method to bind an array of arbitrary data to a Selection. It will return a new Selection that stores the bound data internally and binds every element of the data array to an element of the Selection.

The first `values` argument is an array of values or a function that returns an array of values. With the second optional `key` argument, we can specify a function that identifies each element of the array. The `key` argument is important for D3.js to identify and keep track of the elements for the data joins. Let's first take a look at a simple example:

```
<svg width="400" height="200">
  <circle cx="50" cy="50" r="40" />
  <circle cx="150" cy="50" r="40" />
  <circle cx="250" cy="50" r="40" />
  <circle cx="350" cy="50" r="40" />
</svg>

<script type="text/javascript">
  // Create a data array
  var data = [10, 20, 30, 40];
  // Bind data array to the Selection
  var circles = d3.selectAll('circle').data(data);

 console.log(circles.data());
  // [10, 20, 30, 40]
</script>
```

In the preceding example, we create a data array with four values and a Selection of the 4 circles by d3.selectAll('circle'). Then, we use the .data() function to bind the data to the Selection as well as to retrieve the new Selection afterwards. The action of binding data solely stores the data in the Selection and is not modifying the Selection itself. As we can see in the following screenshot, the resulting HTML page looks the same before and after executing the JavaScript code:

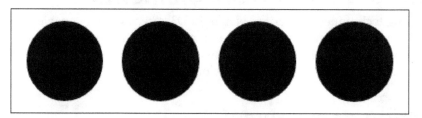

HTML page before and after binding the data

If we bind an array of data with a differing number of elements to a Selection, D3.js will automatically adjust the data to match the Selection, either append undefined values to the data array if it has less elements than the Selection or slice values from the data array if it has more elements than the Selection. We will see what exactly is happening to these values and how to access them in the data join section. Now, we want to look at an example of these adjustments to the bound data, so we extend the code of the previous example with the following code:

```
// Create data arrays
var data_1 = [10, 20];
var data_2 = [10, 20, 30, 40];
var data_3 = [10, 20, 30, 40, 50, 60];

// Bind data_1 to the Selection
circles = d3.selectAll('circle').data(data_1);
console.log(circles.data());
// [10, 20, undefined, undefined]

// Bind data_2 to the Selection
circles = d3.selectAll('circle').data(data_2);
console.log(circles.data());
// [10, 20, 30, 40]

// Bind data_3 to the Selection
circles = d3.selectAll('circle').data(data_3);
console.log(circles.data());
// [10, 20, 30, 40]
```

Using dynamic properties in Selections

Once we bound data to a Selection, we can access this data in attribute and style methods that are applied on a Selection. We achieve this by replacing the value that we want to set with a function similar to `function(d, i) { return d; }`. In this function, the first `d` argument refers to the element in the data array that is bound to the element of the Selection. The second `i` argument refers to the index of the element and the return value of the function serves as the value to set as attribute or style. This concept should become clearer when we look at an example:

```
<svg width="400" height="200">
  <circle cx="50" cy="50" r="40" />
  <circle cx="150" cy="50" r="40" />
  <circle cx="250" cy="50" r="40" />
  <circle cx="350" cy="50" r="40" />
</svg>

<script type="text/javascript">
  // Create a data array
  var data = [10, 20, 30, 40];

  // Bind data array to the Selection
  var circles = d3.selectAll('circle').data(data);

  // Use dynamic properties for the radius
  circles.attr('r', function(d, i) { return d; });
</script>
```

In the preceding code, we bind the `data` array to the `d3.selectAll('circle')` Selection. This returns a new Selection, which we store in the `circles` variable. Now, we can access the values of `data` for each element of `circle` in the `.attr()` function and set the radius of each element depending on the value of the bound data. The concept of referencing attributes of the array elements rather than values is called *dynamic properties*. In the following screenshot, we can see the resulting HTML page after declaring the radius with dynamic properties:

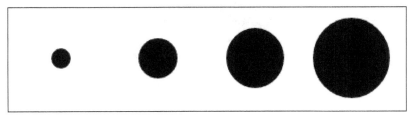

HTML page after applying dynamic properties

Dynamic properties can not only return the current array element, they can also be used to reference properties of the element of an array of objects. Having said that, we can extend the example from before and now bind an array of objects to the Selection:

```
<svg width="400" height="200">

  <circle />
  <circle />
  <circle />
  <circle />
</svg>

<script type="text/javascript">
  // Create a data array containing objects
  var data = [
    {cx:50, cy:50, r: 10, color: '#ff0000'},
    {cx:150, cy:50, r: 20, color: '#ff0066'},
    {cx:250, cy:50, r: 30, color: '#ff00aa'},
    {cx:350, cy:50, r: 40, color: '#ff00ff'}
  ];

  // Bind data array to the Selection
  var circles = d3.selectAll('circle').data(data);

  // Use dynamic properties for the radius
  circles.attr('r', function(d, i) { return d.r; });

  circles
    // Set the stroke color to black
    .attr('stroke', 'black')
    // Set the fill color
    // depending of the bound object
    .attr('fill', function(d, i) { return d.color; })
    // Set the x coordinate of the center
    // depending of the bound object
    .attr('cx', function(d, i) { return d.cx; })
    // Set the y coordinate of the center
    // depending of the bound object
    .attr('cy', function(d, i) { return d.cy; });
</script>
```

In the preceding example, we saw how to dynamically return properties depending on the bound elements of the object array. The d argument in each of the property functions references an element from the array, in this case, an object. In the following figure, we can see the circles after applying the previous dynamic transformations:

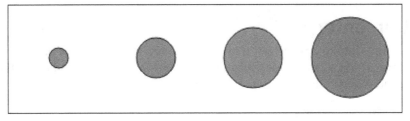

HTML page after applying dynamic properties on an array of objects

If we want to set a property that is dependent on the index, we can use the i argument (the second argument) of the property function:

```
// Set the stroke width
// depending on the index
circles.style('stroke-width', function(d, i) { return i*2; }) ;
```

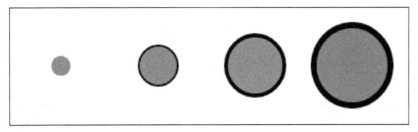

HTML page after applying dynamic properties with index argument

Tracking changes of data with data joins

As we already saw in the previous chapter, data bindings in D3.js are much more powerful than in other DOM transforming libraries. The reason for this is that D3.js implements so called data joins. You learned that due to data joins, D3.js intersects the data array with the Selection while binding the data and provides the developer three subsets of the data array: an enter set, an update set, and an exit set:

- **Enter set**: These are elements of the data array that do not exist in the Selection, so they need to be added

- **Update set**: These are elements of the data array that already exist in the Selection, so they need to be updated

- **Exit set**: These are elements of the Selection that are not in the data array; therefore, to be removed

selection.enter()

Once we bound data to a Selection with the `.data()` method, D3.js provides the `.enter()` and `.exit()` methods to return the enter and exit sets, whereas the update set is returned when calling the Selection itself:

```
<svg width="800" height="500"></svg>
<script type="text/javascript">
var svg = d3.select('svg');
// Get an empty Selection of all circle elements
// and bind a data array to the selection
var circles = svg.selectAll('circles').data([10, 20, 30]);
// Get the enter Selection and append circle elements
circles.enter()
.append('circle');
// The circle elements have been merged to the Selection
circles
.attr('cx', function(d, i) { return (i+1)*100; })
.attr('cy', 50)
.attr('r', function(d) { return d; });
</script>
```

In the previous example, we first load an empty Selection of circle elements. In the second step, we bind the data array [10, 20, 30] to this empty Selection. Then, the `.enter()` method returns all elements from the dataset because none of these elements exist in the Selection. Therefore, we call `.append()` on these elements and create a circle for each data element:

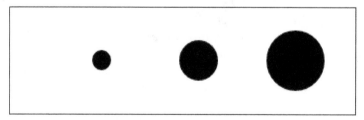

HTML Page after appending elements

Once we use the `.enter()` method to return the enter set, the elements will be internally merged with the update set. Thus, the enter set will be cleared automatically after calling `.enter()`!

selection.exit()

This returns all elements of the Selection that does not exist in the bound data array. Thus, we need to use the `.remove()` method to remove these elements from the DOM and therefore from the Selection. We can extend the previous example with the following lines:

```
// Remove element 30 from the bound data
circles
.data([10, 20])
.exit()
.remove();
```

In the preceding code, we removed the element `30` from the array. Therefore, the `.exit()` method returns exactly this element and we can remove it from the DOM:

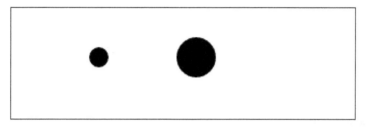

HTML Page after removing one element

Now, the question is where is `selection.update()`?

There is no specific function to return the update set from the Selection because the Selection itself will always return the update set. The data join of an array with three elements, which includes appending, updating, and removing elements is visualized in the following figure:

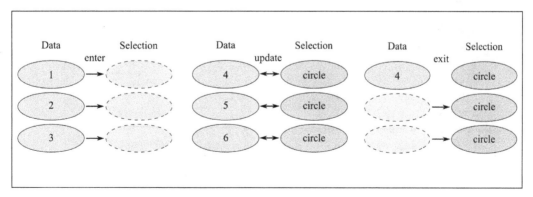

Data joins in D3.js: enter, update and exit

The update pattern

The update pattern illustrates when to update original elements of a Selection, new elements in a Selection, all existing elements of a Selection, and elements that are removed from a Selection. Let's take a look at the implementation:

```
<svg width="800" height="500"></svg>
<script type="text/javascript">
// Create a data array
var data = [];
// Do every 1s
setInterval(function(){
  // Add new random element to data array
  if (data.length < 8) {
    data.push(Math.random());
  }
  else {
    data = [];
  }
  // Redraw the scene
  draw();
}, 1000);
function draw() {
   var svg = d3.select('svg');
// Bind data array to the Selection
  var circles = svg.selectAll('circle').data(data);
  // Update all original elements from the Selection
  circles
    .attr('fill', 'orange');
  // Update all elements, that are new to the Selection
  circles.enter()
    .append('circle')
    .attr('fill', 'red')
    .attr('r', 40)
    .attr('cx', function(d, i) { return i*100 + 50; })
    .attr('cy', 50);
  // Update all elements in the Selection
  circles
    .style('stroke', 'black');
  // Update all elements, that are removed from the Selection
  circles.exit()
    .delay()
    .remove();
}
</script>
```

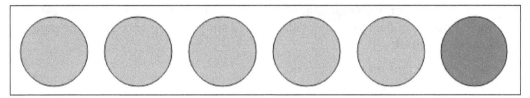

Coloring depending on data join

We observe that in the update pattern, the functions are applied in the following order:

- `selection` to update all original elements
- `selection.enter()` to append all new elements
- `selection` to update all existing elements
- `selection.exit()` to remove all non existing elements

Creating a simple scatter plot

In this chapter, we have so far gathered a lot of knowledge that we want to apply to a real-world application. Let me briefly summarize what you learned so far: creating a Selection of circles, binding an array of data to the Selection, creating new circles if there are new values in the array, and changing their attributes depending on the bound data. These are all the necessary prerequisites to create a first scatter chart. In the following figure, we can already see what we want to create:

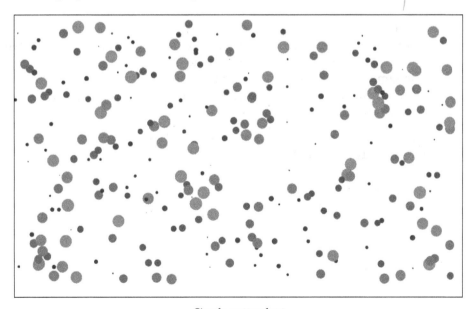

Simple scatter chart

To go one step further, we want to add and delete data points to the chart to use and see the power of data joins. Let's start with a simple setup and create the parent container of the chart:

```
<svg width="800" height="500"></svg>
<script type="text/javascript">
// Our code goes here
</script>
```

Now, we need to create an array of data points that we want to draw. These points can differ in the coordinates of their center point and in the radius of the circles. In the preceding figure, we can also see that we want to color the circles depending on their radius value. We create a function that generates a random data point:

```
function randPoint() {
   var rand = Math.random;
   return { x:rand()*10, y: rand()*10, r: rand()*10 };
}
```
Next, we create an array of data and fill it with random data points.
```
// Create a data array
var data = [];
// Add 300 random elements
for (var i=0; i < 300; i++) {
   data.push(randPoint());
}
```

Now, we have an array of random data points that we want to draw in the following step. To achieve this, we need to create a Selection of circles inside the svg element and bind the data array to this Selection. Due to the fact that we can have multiple points with the same *x* coordinate and multiple points with the same *y* coordinate, we need to set a key function to identify the elements of the bound data. Let's write a key function identifier and bind the data to a selection of circles:

```
// Get the Selection of the svg element
var svg = d3.select('svg');
// Set a key function to identify the elements
function key(d, i) {
   return d.x + '#' + d.y;
}
// Bind data array to the Selection
var circles = svg.selectAll('circle').data(data, key);
```

Now, we create a circle for each new element of the Selection and set its radius and center point coordinates according to the bound data and the canvas size. Then, we color each circle depending on its radius:

```
// Add circles for new data
circles.enter()
.append('circle')
.attr('r', function(d) { return d.r; })
.attr('cx', function(d) { return d.x*70 + 10; })
.attr('cy', function(d) { return d.y*40 + 10; })
.attr('fill', function(d) {
   return 'rgb(' + parseInt(d.r*25) + ',0,0)';
});
```

When running this code, we see that the resulting page looks already like the figure of the scatter chart in the beginning.

Great! However, I want to go one step further and update the chart at a time interval of 150 milliseconds. We want to add new data points, modify existing ones, and remove data points when the values are removed from the bound data. Therefore, we wrap the previous D3-specific code in a draw() function and modify the color filling process of the circle. All circles — also the existing ones — should now adjust their color value. Finally, we will remove the data points when the values are removed from the array. The resulting function should look like this:

```
function draw() {
   // Get the Selection of the svg element
   var svg = d3.select('svg');
   // Set a key function to identify the elements
   function key(d, i) {
      return d.x + '#' + d.y;
}
   // Bind data array to the Selection
   var circles = svg.selectAll('circle').data(data, key);
   // Add circles for new data
   circles.enter()
   .append('circle')
   .attr('r', function(d) { return d.r; })
   .attr('cx', function(d) { return d.x*70 + 10; })
   .attr('cy', function(d) { return d.y*40 + 10; });;
   // Update the color of all circles
   circles
   .attr('fill', function(d) {
      return 'rgb(' + parseInt(d.r*25) + ',0,0)';
   });
```

```
    // Delete circles when removed from data
    circles.exit()
    .remove();
}
```

Now, we can implement a function that adds elements to and removes elements from the array. After modifying the data we need to redraw the image as follows:

```
// Do every 150ms
setInterval(function(){
    // Remove first element from data array
    data.shift();
    // Add new random element to data array
    data.push(randPoint());
    // Redraw the scene
    draw();
}, 150);
```

Now, the scatter chart is automatically updating its data and redrawing itself. In every update, we can observe these three steps:

1. For new values in the data array, circles are generated and their radius and center coordinates are specified.

2. For all values in the Selection, the circles change their fill color depending on the bound data value.

3. For all removed values of the data array, the circles are removed from the scene.

Summary

This chapter gave an introduction to the basic usage of D3.js. You learned how to properly use CSS Selectors to find elements by `name`, `#id`, `.class`, and `[attribute]` in the DOM tree. We saw how to combine selectors with `selector1selector2` by logical AND and with `selector1, selector2` by logical OR, and how to apply hierarchically `selector1 selector2` or by direct ancestors `selector1 > selector2`.

We also discussed how to modify all elements in Selections of HTML and the SVG elements with the usage of the methods `.attr()`, `.style()`, `.property()`, `.text()`, and so on. It's important to remember that most of the time we will use the `.append()` function to insert new elements to a Selection.

Later in this chapter, we learned how to use data binding with D3.js. We used the .data() function to bind data to a Selection and access dynamic properties with a function similar to the (d, i) { return d; } function. In D3.js data, the .enter() and .exit() functions give the developer access to the enter and exit sets of data joins whereas the Selection itself returns the update set. In the last section, we implemented an autoupdating chart that displays random values with circle elements of different center point coordinates, radius, and fill color.

In the next chapter, you will learn how to manipulate data and arrays in D3.js. This will help us to automatically scale the scatter chart and to retrieve statistical values of the data arrays. Later, we will discuss date and time formats in D3.js and use this knowledge to extend the chart such that it displays time series data instead of data points with *x* and *y* coordinates.

3
Manipulating Data

In this chapter, you will learn how to manipulate data in order to preprocess it for visualization and to extract statistical information.

We will start with discussing arrays and array functions in general because this is the canonical representation of data in D3.js. The presented techniques for array manipulation will form a basic toolset to extract relevant data for the visualization and to transform and adapt the structures of flat datasets.

In the following section, we will see very useful string formatting techniques. You will learn how to format numbers on one hand and dates and times on the other hand.

Then, we will discuss scales for numbers, strings, and times in order to map datasets to specific ranges, for example, to linear, logarithmic, or time ranges.

In the last section, we will see the built-in representation for axes in D3.js. With the previously seen techniques, we will be able to construct axes that automatically scale and format the data according to our needs. We will extend the example from the previous chapter, plot time series data and axes and automatically scale the data to these axes.

In this chapter you will learn:

- How to extract statistical information out of arrays
- How to reorganize arrays and associative arrays
- How to group associative arrays
- How to format numbers, dates, and times
- How to use scales to map an input domain to an output range
- How to construct and draw axes
- How to draw time series data

Manipulating datasets in arrays

In data visualizations, we will usually not display the raw data itself, but moreover aggregate and preprocess the data beforehand. Let me give you an example. You are given the access log from a web server that stores every single visitor with his IP address and user agent (a string that contains information about the browser). Rather than plotting all these rows on its own, you may want to sum up all visitors per minute (or per day) and plot a time series histogram of these sums. Or maybe, you want to group the data by different properties, for example, plotting visitors from Europe vs visitors from North America. It is important to know that your ability of plotting this aggregated data is directly dependent on your ability to manipulate datasets.

Most visualizations are backed by data that is stored in arrays. These datasets, for example, consist of simple arrays, associative arrays, or even nested maps. In many cases, the data that we want to visualize comes from different sources; therefore, it has different formats and structures. Thus, we need array manipulations as a preprocessing step.

Working with arrays of data often requires additional methods that can be applied to the whole dataset. These are typically all statistical functions, order and sorting functions, or data transforming functions (such as scaling).

JavaScript and D3.js provide useful functions for array manipulations and transformations. We will go through the most important array manipulation techniques in this section. It might seem a little boring to go through a list of functions, but it enables you to adapt data in all different representations to your needs. In general, the more control you have over the data, the more flexible you are with creating a visualization of the data.

Built-in JavaScript array methods

In general, data manipulation and data processing for visualizations is mostly done with the use of arrays. Thus, the canonical representation of data in D3.js is also an array. JavaScript provides a rich set of native **array mutator** (manipulate arrays), **accessor** (access array values), and **iterator** (loop through arrays) methods that one has to know before continuing with D3.js.

Mutator functions:

- `array.pop()`: This removes and returns the last element from an array
- `array.push(value[, value[, ...]])`: This adds elements to an array after its last element
- `array.reverse()`: This reverses the order of elements in an array and returns the reversed array

- `array.shift()`: This removes and returns the first element of an array
- `array.sort([comparator])`: This sorts the elements of an array by a comparator function and returns the sorted array
- `array.splice(array[, accessor])`: This replaces the elements of an array and returns the new array
- `array.unshift(value[, value[, ...]])`: This adds elements to the beginning of an array

Accessor functions:

- `array.concat(value[, value[, ...]])`: This concatenates an array with other elements or arrays and returns the new array
- `array.join([separator])`: This combines all elements of the array to a string in which the elements will be separated by a separator
- `array.slice([begin[, end]])`: This extracts and returns a range of elements from an array
- `array.indexOf(value[, fromIndex])`: This returns the index of the first occurrence and the value in the array
- `array.lastIndexOf(value[, fromIndex])`: This returns the index of the last occurrence and the value in the array

Iterator functions:

- `array.filter(callback)`: This returns a new array containing elements from the original array whose callback returns `true`
- `array.forEach(callback)`: This calls the callback function for each element
- `array.every(callback)`: This returns true if the callback for every element returns `true`
- `array.map(callback)`: This returns an array containing values returned by the callback for each element
- `array.some(callback)`: This returns true even if a single callback returns `true`
- `array.reduce(callback [, initialValue])`: This applies a callback function on each element of an array where the result of the last callback is provided as an argument (left to right)
- `array.reduceRight(callback)`: This is the same as `array.reduce()`, whereas the array is iterated in the reverse order (right to left)

If you do not know how to use some of the previous functions, I encourage you to look these functions up and learn them properly. They will be very useful every time you have to work on arrays. Believe me, this will happen often in this book, especially mutator methods will be important to add data to arrays and retrieve data from arrays; whereas map and reduce functions will be very useful for statistical computations.

Let me just explain to you three of the above functions that are very useful in data processing and visualization: `array.filter(callback)`, `array.map(callback)`, and `array.reduce(callback)`.

array.filter(callback)

As described previously, the filter function returns a new array that contains a subset of the original array for which the `callback` function returns `true`. Let's try this and return a list of people who are older than 26:

```
var data = [
  {name: 'Ben', age: 27},
  {name: 'Flo', age: 22},
  {name: 'Phil', age: 28},
  {name: 'Chris', age: 26}
];

var filtered = data.filter(function(d){
  return d.age > 26 ?
});

console.log(filtered);
// [{name: 'Ben', age: 27}, {name: 'Phil', age: 28}]
```

array.map(callback)

As described before, the map function executes the `callback` function on every element of an array and returns a new array with all the values of the `callback` functions. Let's transform an array of objects to an array of strings by solely returning the name of every element as follows:

```
var data = [
  {name: 'Ben', age: 27},
  {name: 'Flo', age: 22},
  {name: 'Phil', age: 28},
  {name: 'Chris', age: 26}
];
```

```
var mapped = data.map(function(d){
  return d.name;
});

console.log(mapped);
// ["Ben", "Flo", "Phil", "Chris"]
```

From the previous example, the function of `map` should be clear; it's calling the `callback` function for every element. Let's look at a slightly different example where we now pass an existing function as argument:

```
var data = [9, 16, 25];

var mapped = data.map(Math.sqrt);
console.log(mapped);
// [3, 4, 5]
```

array.reduce(callback [, initialValue])

As described previously, reduce is calling the `callback` function on each element of an array and also providing the result of the previous callback. Then, it returns the result of the last `callback` function. It's often used to sum properties over an array of objects.

Let's compute the sum of the people's ages using the reduce function. Don't forget to add an initial value of 0 so that the d argument always contains the current element; otherwise, the `prev` argument will contain the first element on the first iteration as follows:

```
var data = [
  {name: 'Ben', age: 27},
  {name: 'Flo', age: 22},
  {name: 'Phil', age: 28},
  {name: 'Chris', age: 26}
];

var total = data.reduce(function(prev, d, i, array){
  return prev + d.age;
}, 0);

console.log(total);
// 103
```

More array manipulation with D3.js

D3.js provides a variety of functions to extract statistical information from a dataset and operators to manipulate arrays. We will use the former to extract additional information of the data — for example, to scale the axis to the maximum value of the dataset — and the latter to preprocess the data.

I will discuss a selection of the most useful statistic functions and array transformations.

 Refer to the D3.js wiki link at `https://github.com/mbostock/d3/wiki/Arrays` to explore all the available array manipulation functions.

The following is the list of statistics:

- `d3.min(array[, accessor])`
- `d3.max(array[, accessor])`
- `d3.sum(array[, accessor])`
- `d3.mean(array[, accessor])`
- `d3.median(array[, accessor])`

The following are the operators:

- `d3.shuffle(array)`
- `d3.permute(array, indexes)`
- `d3.merge(array)`
- `d3.range([start, ]stop[, step])`
- `d3.zip(array, array, …)`
- `d3.pairs(array)`

The following are the associatives:

- `d3.keys(object)`
- `d3.values(object)`
- `d3.entries(object)`

The statistic functions take an accessor function as a second optional argument. This function is used to map the array to a new modified array — equivalent to the `array.map(accessor)` operation — before computing the statistic values of the array.

d3.min(array[, accessor])

This function returns the minimum value of an array in natural order, whereas undefined values are ignored, as shown in the following code:

```
var data = [1, 3, 5];

// Min Number
console.log(d3.min(data));
// 1

// Min of square with Accessor
console.log(d3.min(data, function(d) { return d*d; }));
// 1
```

d3.max(array[, accessor])

This function returns the maximum value of an array in natural order, whereas undefined values are ignored as follows:

```
var data = [1, 3, 5];

// Min Number
console.log(d3.max(data));
// 5

// Max of square with Accessor
console.log(d3.max(data, function(d) { return d*d; }));
// 25
```

d3.sum(array[, accessor])

This function returns the sum of the values, whereas strings are parsed as numbers and undefined values and NaN values are ignored, as shown in the following code:

```
var data = [1, 3, 5];

// Sum of Numbers
console.log(d3.sum(data));
// 9

// Sum of square with Accessor
console.log(d3.sum(data, function(d) { return d*d; }));
// 35
```

d3.mean(array[, accessor])

This function returns the mean value of an array, whereas strings are parsed as numbers and undefined values and NaN values are ignored as follows:

```
var data = [1, 3, 5];

// Mean of Numbers
console.log(d3.mean(data));
// 3

// Mean of square with Accessor
console.log(d3.mean(data, function(d) { return d*d; }));
// 11.66
```

d3.median(array[, accessor])

This function returns the median value of an array, whereas undefined values and NaN values are ignored. If the array contains one or more number values, it will return the median of the number values and parse all strings to numbers. If the array contains solely strings, it will return the median string of the array:

```
var data = [1, 3, 5, 6, 10];

// Median of Numbers
console.log(d3.median(data));
// 5


// Median of square with Accessor
console.log(d3.median(data, function(d) { return d*d; }));
// 25
```

d3.shuffle(array)

This function shuffles the order of the elements of array randomly:

```
var data = [1, 3, 5, 6, 10];

// Shuffle the array
d3.shuffle(data)

console.log(data);
// [3, 1, 10, 6, 5]
```

It's not straightforward to seed the pseudorandom generator in JavaScript and make random experiments repeatable. Other projects like `https://github.com/Dashed/ javascript-seed-project` tackle this by overriding the built-in `Math.random()` function.

d3.permute(array, indexes)

This function returns a new array with a permutation of the elements in `array` according to the `indexes` (an array of integer values), as shown in the following code:

```
var values = [124, 643, 321, 346, 163, 239];

// Return a permutation of values
console.log(d3.permute(values, [0, 2, 1, 3, 5, 4, 0, 1]));
// [124, 321, 643, 346, 239, 163, 124, 643]
```

d3.merge(array)

This function combines the elements of `array` with a new array and returns it as follows:

```
var data_1 = [1, 3, 5];
var data_2 = [6, 7, 8];
var data_3 = ["abc", "def", "ghi"];

// Merge the first 2 arrays
console.log(d3.merge([data_1, data_2]));
// [1, 3, 5, 6, 7, 8]

// Merge all arrays
console.log(d3.merge([data_1, data_2, data_3]));
// [1, 3, 5, 6, 7, 8, "abc", "def", "ghi"]
```

d3.range([start,]stop[, step)

This function returns a new array of numbers whose values start with `start` (default is 0) and increase by `step` (default is 1) until `stop`, whereas `stop` is not included in the range:

```
// Generate a range from 0 to 5
console.log(d3.range(5));
// [0, 1, 2, 3, 4]
```

```
// Generate a range from 10 to 20 with a step of 2
console.log(d3.range(10, 20, 2));
// [10, 12, 14, 16, 18]

// Generate a range from 10 to 0
console.log(d3.range(10, 0, -1));
// [10, 9, 8, 7, 6, 5, 4, 3, 2, 1]
```

d3.zip(array, array, ...)

This function returns a new array where the elements from the array arguments are piecewise combined together, as shown in the following code:

```
var keys = [1, 2, 3, 4, 5];
var values = [124, 643, 321, 346, 163];
var colors = ["red", "blue", "green", "purple", "pink"];

// Zip the Values
console.log(d3.zip(keys, values, colors));
// [[1,124,"red"], [2,643,"blue"], [3,321,"green"],
//  [4,346,"purple"], [5,163,"pink"]]
```

d3.pairs(array)

This function combines every subsequent elements of array to a pair of 2 elements and returns them as a new array:

```
var values = [124, 643, 321, 346, 163, 239];

// Group the values in pairs of 2
console.log(d3.pairs(values));
// [[124,643], [643,321], [321,346], [346,163], [163,239]]
```

d3.keys(object)

This function returns an array of the keys from object:

```
var values = {
  name: "Peter", age: 25, gender: "male", eyes: "brown"
};

// Extract the Keys
console.log(d3.keys(values));
// ["name", "age", "gender", "eyes"]
```

d3.values(object)

This function returns an array of the values from `object`:

```
var values = {
  name: "Peter", age: 25, gender: "male", eyes: "brown"
};

// Extract the Values
console.log(d3.values(values));
// ["Peter", 25, "male", "brown"]
```

d3.entries(object)

This function returns an array of objects that contain the keys and values from `object`:

```
var values = {
  name: "Peter", age: 25, gender: "male", eyes: "brown"
};

// Extract the Entries
console.log(d3.entries(values));
// [{key:"name", value:"Peter"},
//  {key:"age", value:25},
//  {key:"gender", value:"male"},
//  {key:"eyes", value:"brown"}]
```

Grouping elements with d3.nest

Often, the visualization data is loaded from flat-structured sources such as comma-separated lists, but contains hierarchical-structured data. Let me give you an example. Let's look at the access log of a web server that consists of a list of visitors. Each entry stores the user agent (detailed information about the browser of a visitor) as a string, whereas this string contains data about the used browsers. We immediately see that all visitors using a Chrome browser or all visitors from Europe are somehow related. In our mind, we can easily create a hierarchical tree structure, where every branch of this tree contains visitors from different browsers: one branch for Chrome, one branch for Safari, and so on. However, the flat-structured file does not provide access to this hierarchical structure.

In D3.js, it's very easy to create nested tree structures of flat datasets with the d3.nest() operator. This operator also allows multiple levels of hierarchical groups; in order to create such a group, we use the .key() function. The different levels can also be sorted with the .sortKeys() function. Let's look at an example:

```
var values = [
    {n: "Peter", age: 25, gender: "male", eyes: "brown"},
    {n: "Linda", age: 22, gender: "female", eyes: "brown"},
    {n: "Susi", age: 28, gender: "female", eyes: "blue"},
    {n: "Hans", age: 36, gender: "male", eyes: "green"},
    {n: "Carine", age: 42, gender: "female", eyes: "brown"},
    {n: "Fred", age: 47, gender: "male", eyes: "brown"},
    {n: "Philipp", age: 19, gender: "male", eyes: "brown"},
    {n: "Flo", age: 34, gender: "male", eyes: "blue"}
];

var sorted_values = d3.nest()
    // Group by property gender (male, female) on 1. level
    .key(function(d) { return d.gender; })
    // Sort 1. level keys with descending order
    .sortKeys(d3.descending)
    // Group by property ages (10, 20, 30, 40, 50) on 2. level
    .key(function(d) { return Math.floor(d.age / 10) * 10; })
    // Sort 2. level keys with ascending order
    .sortKeys(d3.ascending)
    // Add the dataset
    .entries(values);
```

Applying the nest operator on the flat data structure in the preceding example will create a hierarchical-structured object that looks like this:

```
[
    { key: 'male', values: [
        { key: 10, values: [
            {n: "Philipp", age: 19, gender: "male", eyes: "brown"}
        ]
        },
        { key: 20, values: [
            {n: "Peter", age: 25, gender: "male", eyes: "brown"},
        ]
        },
        { key: 30, values: [
            {n: "Hans", age: 36, gender: "male", eyes: "green"},
            {n: "Flo", age: 34, gender: "male", eyes: "blue"}
        ]
```

```
      },
      { key: 40, values: [
        {n: "Fred", age: 47, gender: "male", eyes: "brown"}
      ]
      },
    ]
  },
  { key: 'female', values: [
    { key: 20, values: [
      {n: "Linda", age: 22, gender: "female", eyes: "brown"},
      {n: "Susi", age: 28, gender: "female", eyes: "blue"}
    ]
    },
    { key: 40, values: [
      {n: "Carine", age: 42, gender: "female", eyes: "brown"}
    ]
    },
  ]
  },
]
```

D3.js provides two comparator functions: d3.ascending and d3.descending. One can easily implement a custom comparator function, for example, take a look at the following code to compare strings by its length:

```
var custom_comp = function(a, b) {
  return a.length < b.length ? -1 : a.length >
b.length
    ? 1
    : 0;
}
```

Formatting numbers and dates

In visualizations, we will often be confronted with labeling our data properly and make the values easy to read. Floating point divisions often return ugly and long decimal numbers that do not have to be displayed with the very last position after the decimal point. When displaying time series data, we often want to customize the label captions such that they just display, for example, the current day, month, or year. You will first learn about number formats in D3.js and afterwards take a look at date and time formatting.

Specifying a number format

To create a custom number formatting function — that formats a number to a string — we use the d3.format(specifier) helper function. As an argument, we will specify the format of the output. This will return a custom function that takes the number as an argument and returns the formatted output.

The specifier has the following form:

```
[[fill]align][sign][symbol][0][width][,][.precision][type]
```

Normally, we would first define a formatter function and then apply it to the numbers that we want to format, similar to the following example:

```
// Create Formatter function
var formatter = d3.format('e');

// Apply Formatter function to number
console.log(formatter(0.3123));
// "3.123e-1"
```

However, in the following examples, I will call the result of d3.format() directly as a new function in order to make the examples more readable and comparable.

Types of formatting

In D3.js, we can use the following types to format number values:

- e: Exponent
- g: General
- f: Fixed
- d: Integer
- r: Rounded to precision if specified
- %: Percentage
- p: Percentage rounded to precision if specified
- b: Binary
- o: Octal
- x: Hexadecimal
- X: Hexadecimal with uppercase letters
- c: Unicode character
- s: SI-suffixed and rounded

Let's look at some examples:

```
console.log(d3.format('e')(0.3123));       // "3.123e-1"
console.log(d3.format('g')(31.223e3));     // "31223"
console.log(d3.format('f')(31.23));        // "31"
console.log(d3.format('d')(124));          // "124"
console.log(d3.format('r')(31.53));        // "31.53"
console.log(d3.format('%')(0.23));         // "23%"
console.log(d3.format('p')(0.2314));       // "23.14%"
console.log(d3.format('b')(23));           // "10111"
console.log(d3.format('o')(32));           // "40"
console.log(d3.format('x')(59));           // "3b"
console.log(d3.format('X')(63));           // "3F"
console.log(d3.format('c')(81));           // "Q"
console.log(d3.format('s')(31.223e3));     // "31.223k"
```

Precision

The precision of the decimal number can be defined with the .precision notation. Let's look at some examples:

```
console.log(d3.format('.2e')(0.3123));     // "3.12e-1"
console.log(d3.format('.2f')(31.23213));   // "31.23"
```

Thousands separator

The thousands separator can be enabled by placing a comma in front of the precision. By default, D3.js uses a comma as a separator.

 To change the default localization of D3.js, one can declare a new custom locale. More information on how to customize a locale can be found in the wiki link at https://github. com/mbostock/d3/wiki/Localization.

Let's take a quick look at an example:

```
console.log(d3.format(',')(31231.23213));    // "31,231.23213"
console.log(d3.format(',.2f')(31231.23213)); // "31,231.23"
```

Width

The width property specifies the minimum length of the formatted string. In the following example, we can see that both strings have the same length:

```
console.log(d3.format('9.2e')(31231.23213));   // "  3.12e+4"
console.log(d3.format('9,.2f')(31231.23213));  // "31,231.23"
```

Zero padding

All spaces that are added with the width property can be set to 0 with the zero padding options. As we can see in the example, this can be activated via the 0 string in the number format:

```
console.log(d3.format('09.2e')(31231.23213));    // "003.12e+4"
console.log(d3.format('09,.2f')(31231.23213));   // "31,231.23"
```

The currency symbol

We can easily add currency symbols or a base suffix with the symbol property. To use custom currency symbols, they need to be defined in a locale, which is similar to the thousands separator. Let's look at a standard example:

```
console.log(d3.format('#8b')(164));        // "0b10100100 "
console.log(d3.format('$.2e')(331.213));   // "$3.31e+2"
```

Signs

We can define the utilization of signs with the following options:

- +: This sign is used for positive and negative numbers
- -: This sign is used solely for negative numbers
- ' ': This is used as a space for positive numbers and a sign for negative ones

Let's see some examples:

```
console.log(d3.format('.2f')(331.213));     // "331.21"
console.log(d3.format('.2f')(-331.213));    // "-331.21"
console.log(d3.format('+.2f')(331.213));    // "+331.21"
console.log(d3.format('+.2f')(-331.213));   // "-331.21"
console.log(d3.format('-.2f')(331.213));    // "331.21"
console.log(d3.format('-.2f')(-331.213));   // "-331.21"
console.log(d3.format(' .2f')(331.213));    // " 331.21"
console.log(d3.format(' .2f')(-331.213));   // "-331.21"
```

The align property

We can define the alignment of the number in the string with the following options:

- <: This is used for left aligning
- >: This is used for right aligning
- ^: This is used for center aligning

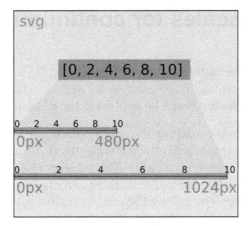

Mapping the dataset to a pixel range

D3.js provides a very useful tool to map a dataset to a certain range of pixels: d3.scale. In D3.js, we call the mapping function's scale, the slice of the dataset that we want to map the domain to, and the pixel range on which we want to map the dataset range. In the following figure, we can see a dataset, where only the positive values are mapped to the width of the axis:

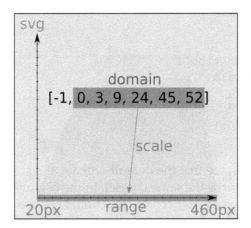

Visualizing a scale

In order to represent different data types with scales, we distinguish between *quantitative scales* for continuous data such as numbers ([1, 2, 3, 4, ...]), *ordinal scales* for discrete data such as strings (["small", "medium", "big", ...]), and *time scales* for time data ([Date, Date, Date, ...]).

Quantitative scales for continuous data (numbers)

There are a variety of quantitative scales implemented in D3.js, for example, linear scales, power scales, logarithmic scales, and so on. In this section, we will solely discuss linear scales because the methods can be applied in the same way to other scales.

A `scale` can be constructed by calling the corresponding scale constructor, in this case, `d3.scale.linear()`; this will return a scale object. To apply the scale, we can simply call the `scale(x)` object on a value. This operation will map the x value to a pixel value. We can also apply the opposite transformation — mapping a pixel value to a value from the dataset — by calling the `scale.invert(y)` function. However first, let's construct such a scale and apply it to some data:

```
var scale = d3.scale.linear();
```

This will return the scale object for a default domain of values `[0, 1]` and a default range of pixels `[0, 1]`. This means that it will map the values `[0, 1]` to `[0, 1]`. Therefore, it's not surprising that if we scale all values from an array using this default domain and scale, the resulting array will be exactly the same as the input dataset:

```
var data_in = [1, 3, 5];
var data_out = [];

data_in.forEach(function(d){
  data_out.push(scale(d));
});

console.log(data_out);
// [1, 3, 5]
```

In the above code, we can see that the default domain and scale is not very fascinating because it returns the same dataset. In the beginning of this chapter, we talked about the native `array.map(func)` function. Let's use this function to write the preceding code a little more compact:

```
console.log([1, 3, 5].map(scale));
// [1, 3, 5]
```

Wow, that's much shorter! Let's move on to look at some examples of how we can modify the scale object:

- `scale.domain([numbers])`
- `scale.range([values])`
- `scale.clamp([boolean])`

- `scale.nice([count])`
- `scale.ticks([count])`
- `scale.tickFormat(count, [format])`

scale.domain([numbers])

We can define the domain of the dataset by passing an array of two (or more) values as an argument. Let's see an example, where we map the domain `[0, 10]` to the default range of `[0, 1]` as follows:

```
var scale = d3.scale.linear().domain([0, 10]);
console.log([1, 3, 5].map(scale));// [0.1, 0.3, 0.5]
```

We observe that all values from the dataset get divided by the factor 10. This makes absolute sense as we are mapping values from `[0, 10]` to a range of `[0, 1]`.

 If we pass an array of more than two values as an argument, we construct a *polylinear* scale for which we also need the same number of elements in the range.

scale.range([numbers])

We can define the range of the scale by passing an array of two (or more) values as an argument. Let's see an example, where we map the domain `[0, 10]` to a range of `[0, 100]`:

```
var scale = d3.scale.linear()
  .domain([0, 10])
  .range([0, 100]);
console.log([1, 3, 5].map(scale));// [10, 30, 50]
```

We can see that all values are multiplied by a factor 10, as we expected from mapping `[0, 10]` to a range of `[0, 100]`.

If we define more than two numbers, we construct a *polylinear* scale. An example will look like this:

```
var scale = d3.scale.linear()
  .domain([-1, 0, 1])
  .range([0, 50, 100]);
console.log([[-0.5, 0.2, 0.8].map(scale));// [25, 60, 90]
```

scale.clamp([boolean])

It might look a little strange in the previous examples, where we mapped values from the dataset [1, 3, 5] that are not inside the defined domain of [0, 1]. The reason for this is that D3.js scales do not clamp the data by default. This clamping behavior can be enabled by setting scale.clamp(true). Then, range values are computed only if the x value is inside the input domain and otherwise just replaced with the minimum or maximum range value. We can see this behavior in the following example:

```
var scale = d3.scale.linear()
  .domain([0, 3])
  .range([0, 300])
  .clamp(true);
console.log([1, 3, 5].map(scale));// [100, 300, 300]
```

scale.nice([count])

The .nice() method extends the input domain such that the starting and ending values are nicely rounded values. If a count argument is specified, it takes the step sizes for count number of ticks (see next section) into account:

```
var scale = d3.scale.linear()
  .domain([0.112, 3.123])
  .range([0, 50])
  .nice(3);
console.log([1, 3, 5].map(scale));
// [12.5, 37.5, 62.5]
```

scale.ticks([count])

The .ticks() method returns approximately count (default is 10) values in between the input domain. Let's look at an example:

```
var scale = d3.scale.linear()
  .domain([0, 5])
  .range([0, 100]);

console.log(scale.ticks());
// [0, 0.5, 1, 1.5, 2, 2.5, 3, 3.5, 4, 4.5, 5]

console.log(scale.ticks(5));
// [0, 1, 2, 3, 4, 5]
```

scale.tickFormat(count [,specifier])

This sets a format defined by `specifier` for the tick values with the `.tickFormat()` method, as shown in the following code:

```
var scale = d3.scale.linear()
  .domain([0, 1])
  .range([0, 100]);

var ticks_formatter = scale.tickFormat(5, "%");

console.log(scale.ticks(5).map(ticks_formatter));
// ["0%", "20%", "40%", "60%", "80%", "100%"]
```

Ordinal scales for discrete data (strings)

Similar to quantitative scales, we can map discrete input values to a defined output domain in ordinal scales. Now, we need to define a domain of discrete input values (such as strings) and map each of them to an output range. Let's take a look at an example:

```
var scale = d3.scale.ordinal()
  .domain(["A", "B", "C", "D", "E", "F"])
  .range([0, 1, 2, 3, 4, 5]);

console.log(["A", "B", "C"].map(scale));
// [0, 1, 2]
```

In addition to the linear scale methods, we will add the following useful functions to compute dimensions for discrete values:

- `scale.rangePoints(interval[, padding])`
- `scale.rangeBands(interval[, padding[, outerPadding]])`
- `scale.rangeBand()`
- `scale.rangeExtent()`

scale.rangePoints(interval [, padding])

The `scale.rangePoints()` method computes a range to draw data points, which is often used in plotting discrete functions. The range in `interval` is divided by the number of elements in the domain and adds `padding` to each element. Let's look at the following example:

```
var scale = d3.scale.ordinal()
  .domain(["A", "B", "C", "D", "E", "F"])
  .rangePoints([0, 100], 0.5);

console.log(scale.range());
// [4.54, 22.72, 40.90, 59.09, 77.27, 95.45]


console.log(["A", "B", "C"].map(scale));
// [4.54, 22.72, 40.90]
```

scale.rangeBands(interval [, padding [, outerPadding]])

The `scale.rangeBands()` method computes a range to draw data bands like in bar charts. The range in `interval` is divided by the number of elements in the domain and adds `padding` and `outerPadding` to each element. Let's look at an example:

```
var scale = d3.scale.ordinal()
  .domain(["A", "B", "C", "D", "E", "F"])
  .rangeBands([0, 100]);

console.log(scale.range());
// [0, 16.66, 33.33, 50, 66.66, 83.33]


console.log(["A", "B", "C"].map(scale));
// [0, 16.66, 33.33]
```

scale.rangeBand()

This returns the width of a single band that was configured with `scale.rangeBands()`. Take a look at the following example:

```
var scale = d3.scale.ordinal()
  .domain(["A", "B", "C", "D", "E", "F"])
  .rangeBands([0, 100], 0.2, 0.1);
```

```
console.log(scale.range());
// [1.66, 18.33, 35, 51.66, 68.33, 85.00]

console.log(scale.rangeBand())
// 13.33
```

scale.rangeExtent()

This returns an array containing the minimum and maximum value of the range that was configured with `scale.rangeBands()`. Let's see an example:

```
var scale = d3.scale.ordinal()
  .domain(["A", "B", "C", "D", "E", "F"])
  .rangeBands([0, 100], 0.2, 0.1);

console.log(scale.range());
// [1.66, 18.33, 35, 51.66, 68.33, 85.00]

console.log(scale.rangeExtent());
// [0, 100]
```

Predefined ordinal color scales

D3.js has various built-in ordinal color scales such as `d3.scale.category10()`, `d3.scale.category20()`, `d3.scale.category20b()`, and `d3.scale.category20c()`. They can be used easily to quickly color discrete sets of values. Here is a simple example of how to use this scale:

```
var scale = d3.scale.category10();

console.log([1,2,3,4,5,6,7,8,9,10].map(scale));
// ["#ff7f0e", "#2ca02c", "#d62728", "#9467bd", "#8c564b",
//  "#e377c2", "#7f7f7f", "#bcbd22", "#17becf", "#1f77b4"]
```

Time scales for time data (date and time)

The time scale extends the linear scale and adds a linear representation of dates and time. It's used very similar to the linear scale with the exception that it takes JavaScript dates as input for the values to be scaled. Also, the arguments for the `scale.domain()` function are now dates. Let's see this in an example:

```
var data = [
  new Date(2015,2,1),
  new Date(2015,4,1),
  new Date(2015,6,1)
```

```
];
var domain = [
    new Date(2015,0,1),
    new Date(2015,11,31)
];

var scale = d3.time.scale()
  .domain(domain)
  .range([0,100]);

console.log(data.map(scale));
// [16.20, 32.95, 49.71]
```

We can also use the built-in d3.time.scale.utc() function to create a time scale with a preconfigured UTC tickFormat.

All about axes

Until now, we just scaled our dataset without drawing a single shape on the screen. For the next step, I want to introduce d3.svg.axis(), a built-in function to draw axes and labels. This function makes it very easy and comfortable to add an axis to a chart, as shown in the following code:

```
var axis = d3.svg.axis();
```

First, we create a new axis object with d3.svg.axis(), which we can then configure by calling different methods on it. I will now discuss the most important of these methods:

- axis.scale([scale]): This adds scaling to an axis as follows:

```
var scale = d3.scale.linear()
  .domain([0, 10])
  .range([0, 100]);

var axis = d3.svg.axis()
  .scale(scale);
```

- axis.orient([orientation]): This specifies an orientation of the ticks values relative to the axis. The orientation can be *top*, *bottom*, *left*, or *right*:

```
var axis = d3.svg.axis()
  .orient('bottom');
```

- `axis.ticks([arguments...])`: This specifies the tick number or interval relative to the given scale, as shown in the following code:

```
var axis = d3.svg.axis()
.ticks(20);

var axis = d3.svg.axis()
.ticks(d3.time.minutes, 15);
```

- `axis.tickValues([values])`: This specifies an array of custom tick values as follows:

```
var axis = d3.svg.axis()
   .tickValues([1, 2, 3, 5, 8, 13, 21]);
```

- `axis.tickFormat([format])`: This sets a format for the tick values specified by a formatting function `format`, as shown in the following code:

```
var axis = d3.svg.axis()
   .tickFormat(d3.format(".3s"));
```

Drawing the axis

Finally, in order to draw the axis, we need to call the `axis` function on a D3-Selection `selection` that serves as axis container. The axis function we generate completes the SVG layout for the axis, including the axis itself, the ticks, and tick labels:

```
var scale = d3.scale.linear()
   .domain([0, 10])
   .range([50, 150]);

var axis = d3.svg.axis()
   .scale(scale);

d3.select('svg').append('g')
   .attr('class', 'axis')
   .call(axis);
```

As we remember from the last chapter, the `selection.call(func)` method executes the `func` function and provides the `selection` object as an argument identical to `func(selection)`.

When we look at the resulting SVG in a browser, we observe that the axis generator function is so smart that it takes the range values from the scale function and translates the axis according to this range, as shown in the following screenshot:

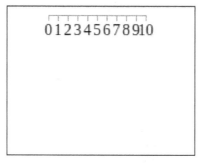

Autogenerated axis

We can see this more clearly if we inspect the element with the developer tools, as shown in the following screenshot:

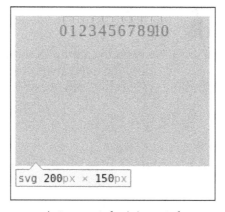

Autogenerated axis inspected

This is very useful and comfortable. We can now generate scales for our dataset and link it with axis and then just autogenerate the complete axis layout.

Adding axes to the scatter chart

Now, we want to apply all this knowledge to a real-world visualization. The aim is to extend the visualization of the previous chapter, which is similar to the following figure of a time series chart. We want to display time series data and implement self updating axes that automatically scales to the maximum values of the dataset.

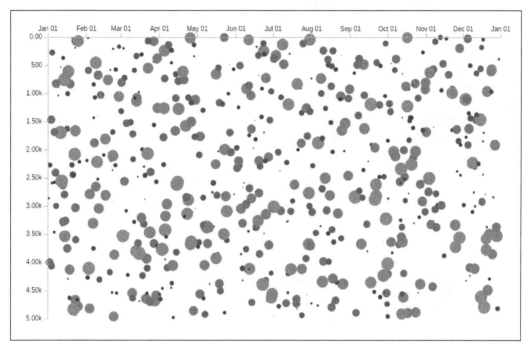

Time series scatter chart

First, we set up our application. We need to create a structure of our svg container, which holds the chart, data values, and the axes. Additionally, we need to define a CSS snippet (which we will use for all visualizations) to render the axis with crisp edges:

```
<style type="text/css">
  .axis path, .axis line {
    fill: none;
    stroke: #999;
    shape-rendering: crispEdges;
  }
  .tick {
    font: 10px sans-serif;
  }
</style>
```

```
<script type="text/javascript">        var width = 800;
  var height = 500;

  // Create the containers
  var svg = d3.select('body').append('svg')
    .attr("width", width)
    .attr("height", height);
  var svg_data = svg.append('g')
    .attr('class', 'data');
  var svg_axis = svg.append('g')
    .attr('class', 'axis');
  var svg_x_axis = svg_axis.append('g')
    .attr('class', 'x-axis');
  var svg_y_axis = svg_axis.append('g')
    .attr('class', 'y-axis');

  // Margins
  var margin = {top: 40, right: 40, bottom: 40, left:60};

  // code continues here
  ...
</script>
```

Then, we create a function that generates a random time series data point between a start and end date as follows:

```
// Domain for values

var start = new Date('2013-01-01');
var end = new Date('2013-12-31');

// Random data point generator
var randPoint = function() {
  var rand = Math.random;
  var rand_time = start.getTime() + rand() * (end.getTime() -
    start.getTime());
  return { x:new Date(rand_time), y: rand()*5000, r: rand()*10
    };
}
```

Next, we create a data array with 300 random data points, as shown in the following code:

```
// Create a data array with 300 random data points
var data = d3.range(300).map(randPoint);
```

Now, let's create a `draw()` function, a function that draws and updates the chart, as shown in the following code:

```
function draw() {
  // code continues here
  . . .
}
```

In this function, we implement two scale functions: one time scale for the x-axis and a linear scale for the y-axis as follows:

```
function draw() {

  var x_scale = d3.time.scale()
    .domain([start, d3.max(data, function(d) { return d.x; })])
    .range([margin.left, width - margin.right])
    .nice();

  var y_scale = d3.scale.linear()
    .domain([0, d3.max(data, function(d) { return d.y; })])
    .range([margin.top, height - margin.bottom])
    .nice();
  . . .
}
```

Now, we can configure and draw the axes; we want the *x* axis to be aligned at the top and the ticks oriented also at the top, whereas we want the *y* axis to be aligned on the left-hand side and the ticks oriented also on the left-hand side. We also need to translate the *x* and *y* axis according to the margins, as shown in the following code:

```
function draw() {
  . . .
  var x_axis = d3.svg.axis()
    .scale(x_scale)
    .orient('top')
    .tickFormat(d3.time.format('%b %d'));

  svg_x_axis
    .attr("transform", "translate(0, " + margin.top + ")")
    .call(x_axis);

  var y_axis = d3.svg.axis()
    .scale(y_scale)
    .orient('left')
    .tickFormat(d3.format(".3s"));
```

```
svg_y_axis
  .attr("transform", "translate(" + margin.left + ")")
  .call(y_axis);
...


}
```

Finally, we can bind the data and add, update, and delete the circle. We should not forget to pass a valid key identifier function that identifies each data point in the chart as follows:

```
function draw() {
  ...
  // Set a key function to identify the elements
  var key = function(d, i) { return d.x + '#' + d.y; }

  // Bind data array to the Selection
  var circles = svg_data.selectAll('circle').data(data, key);

  // update the dataset
  circles

  // Add circles for new data
    .enter()
    .append('circle')

  // Change the properties of all circles
    .attr('r', function(d) { return d.r; })
    .attr('cx', function(d) { return x_scale(d.x); })
    .attr('cy', function(d) { return y_scale(d.y); })
    .attr('fill', function(d, i) {
      return 'rgb(' + parseInt(d.r*25) + ',0,' + parseInt(d.r*25)
        + ')';
    })

  // Delete circles when removed from data
    .exit()
    .remove();
}
```

Then, we want to bring the visualization to life, generate new data points, and delete old data points every 50 milliseconds and update the chart, as shown in the following code:

```
// Do every 50ms
setInterval(function(){
```

```
    // Remove first element from data array
    data.shift();

    // Add new random element to data array
    data.push(randPoint());

    // Redraw the scene
    draw();
  }, 50);
```

The result looks exactly like the image of the time series scatter chart. We can see that due to our configuration of the axes inside the `draw()` function, the chart is automatically adjusting the ranges on the axes according to the maximal values.

Summary

In this chapter, I explained the usage of the most important statistical functions (such as `d3.min()` and `d3.max()`), and we saw them applied in the last example. They are useful to resize the axes and the chart automatically, when values in the dataset are out of the current range of the axis.

We also discussed array manipulation functions, which help us to modify, structure, and preprocess the data for the visualization. In the first section, we also saw an example of `d3.nest()` that groups elements as an associative array by their keys in multihierarchical levels.

You learned how to format number values and convert them to strings with `d3.format()`. The specifier defines how the formatter parses the values and formats them in different data types, currencies, and alignments.

Then, we introduced scales as a way to map an input domain to an output range. We saw linear scales for quantitative and ordinal scales as well as time scales, which are basically linear scales with JavaScript date objects.

In the last section, you learned about drawing axis and putting the previous knowledge all together. This enabled you to extend the demo from the previous chapter such that it displays time series values and auto updates.

In the next chapter, we will include the visualization in an AngularJS application and write our first testable and reusable chart directive.

4
Building a Chart Directive

In the last two chapters, we saw a basic introduction to D3.js and learned about data preprocessing and array manipulation. In this chapter, we will apply the acquired knowledge to integrate a D3.js visualization into a simple AngularJS application.

First, we will set up an AngularJS template that serves as a boilerplate for the examples and the application. We will see a typical directory structure for an AngularJS project and initialize a controller. Similar to the previous example, the controller will generate random data that we want to display in an autoupdating chart.

Next, we will wrap D3.js in a factory and create a directive for the visualization. You will learn how to isolate the components from each other. We will create a simple AngularJS directive and write a custom compile function to create and update the chart.

In the end, you will learn about unit tests, integration tests, set them up, and implement them for the visualization components. This will make the component maintainable and keep it bug free.

In this chapter, you will learn how to:

- Set up a simple AngularJS application
- Integrate D3.js into AngularJS
- Create a visualization directive
- Write unit tests in the visualization component
- Write integration tests for the application

Setting up an AngularJS application

To get started with this chapter, I assume that you feel comfortable with the main concepts of AngularJS: the application structure, controllers, directives, services, dependency injection, and scopes. I will use these concepts without introducing them in great detail, so if you do not know about one of these topics, first try an intermediate AngularJS tutorial or read the recommended literature in *Chapter 1, The Magic of SVG, D3.js, and AngularJS.*

Organizing the directory

To begin with, we will create a simple AngularJS boilerplate for the examples and the visualization application. We will use this boilerplate during the development of the sample application throughout the book. Let's create a project root directory that contains the following files and folders:

- `bower_components/`: This directory contains all third-party components
- `src/`: This directory contains all source files
- `src/app.js`: This file contains source of the application
- `src/app.css`: CSS layout of the application
- `test/`: This directory contains all test files (`test/config/` contains all test configurations, `test/spec/` contains all unit tests, and `test/e2e/` contains all integration tests)
- `index.html`: This is the starting point of the application

Installing AngularJS

In this book, we use the AngularJS version 1.3.14, but different patch versions (~1.3.0) should also work fine with the examples. Let's first install AngularJS with the Bower package manager. Therefore, we execute the following command in the root directory of the project:

```
bower install angular#1.3.14
```

Now, AngularJS is downloaded and installed to the `bower_components/` directory. If you don't want to use Bower, you can also simply download the source files from the AngularJS website and put them in a `libs/` directory.

 Note that—if you develop large AngularJS applications—you most likely want to create a separate `bower.json` file and keep track of all your third-party dependencies.

Bootstrapping the index file

We can move on to the next step and code the index.html file that serves as a starting point for the application and all examples of this section. We need to include the JavaScript application files and the corresponding CSS layouts, the same for the chart component. Then, we need to initialize AngularJS by placing an ng-app attribute to the html tag; this will create the root scope of the application. In this book, we will call the AngularJS application myApp, as shown in the following code:

```html
<html ng-app="myApp">
  <head>
    <!-- Include 3rd party libraries -->
    <script src="bower_components/d3/d3.js" charset="UTF-
8"></script>
    <script src="bower_components/angular/angular.js"
    charset="UTF-8"></script>

    <!-- Include the application files -->
    <script src="src/app.js"></script>
    <link href="src/app.css" rel="stylesheet">

    <!-- Include the files of the chart component -->
    <script src="src/chart.js"></script>
    <link href="src/chart.css" rel="stylesheet">

  </head>
  <body>
    <!-- AngularJS example go here  -->
  </body>
</html>
```

For all the examples in this section, I will use the exact same setup as the preceding code. I will only change the body of the HTML page or the JavaScript or CSS sources of the application. I will indicate to which file the code belongs to with a comment for each code snippet.

 If you are not using Bower and previously downloaded D3.js and AngularJS in a libs/ directory, refer to this directory when including the JavaScript files.

Adding a module and a controller

Next, we initialize the AngularJS module in the `app.js` file and create a main controller for the application. The controller should create random data (that represent some simple logs) in a fixed interval. Let's generate some random number of visitors every second and store all data points on the scope as follows:

```
/* src/app.js */
// Application Module
angular.module('myApp', [])

// Main application controller
.controller('MainCtrl', ['$scope', '$interval',
  function ($scope, $interval) {

    var time = new Date('2014-01-01 00:00:00 +0100');

    // Random data point generator
    var randPoint = function() {
      var rand = Math.random;
      return { time: time.toString(), visitors: rand()*100 };
    }

    // We store a list of logs
    $scope.logs = [ randPoint() ];

    $interval(function() {
      time.setSeconds(time.getSeconds() + 1);
      $scope.logs.push(randPoint());
    }, 1000);
}]);
```

In the preceding example, we define an array of logs on the scope that we initialize with a random point. Every second, we will push a new random point to the logs. The points contain a number of visitors and a timestamp—starting with the date `2014-01-01 00:00:00` (timezone GMT+01) and counting up a second on each iteration. I want to keep it simple for now; therefore, we will use just a very basic example of random access log entries. Later in this book, we will use the `socket.io` library to push a list of real logs from our server applications directly to the AngularJS application in real time.

 Consider to use the cleaner *controller as* syntax for larger AngularJS applications because it makes the scopes in HTML templates explicit! However, for compatibility reasons, I will use the standard controller and `$scope` notation.

Integrating D3.js into AngularJS

We bootstrapped a simple AngularJS application in the previous section. Now, the goal is to integrate a D3.js component seamlessly into an AngularJS application—in an Angular way. This means that we have to design the AngularJS application and the visualization component such that the modules are fully encapsulated and reusable. In order to do so, we will use a separation on different levels:

- Code of different components goes into different files
- Code of the visualization library goes into a separate module
- Inside a module, we divide logics into controllers, services, and directives

Using this clear separation allows you to keep files and modules organized and clean. If at anytime we want to replace the D3.js backend with a canvas pixel graphic, we can just implement it without interfering with the main application. This means that we want to use a new module of the visualization component and dependency injection.

These modules enable us to have full control of the separate visualization component without touching the main application and they will make the component maintainable, reusable, and testable.

Organizing the directory

First, we add the new files for the visualization component to the project:

- `src/`: This is the default directory to store all the file components for the project
- `src/chart.js`: This is the JS source of the chart component
- `src/chart.css`: This is the CSS layout for the chart component
- `test/test/config/`: This directory contains all test configurations
- `test/spec/test/spec/chart.spec.js`: This file contains the unit tests of the chart component
- `test/e2e/chart.e2e.js`: This file contains the integration tests of the chart component

 If you develop large AngularJS applications, this is probably not the folder structure that you are aiming for. Especially in bigger applications, you will most likely want to have components in separate folders and directives and services in separate files.

Then, we will encapsulate the visualization from the main application and create the new `myChart` module for it. This will make it possible to inject the visualization component or parts of it — for example just the chart directive — to the main application.

Wrapping D3.js

In this module, we will wrap D3.js — which is available via the global `d3` variable — in a *service*; actually, we will use a *factory* to just return the reference to the `d3` variable. This enables us to pass D3.js as a dependency inside the newly created module wherever we need it. The advantage of doing so is that the injectable `d3` component — or some parts of it — can be mocked for testing easily.

Let's assume we are loading data from a remote resource and do not want to wait for the time to load the resource every time we test the component. Then, the fact that we can mock and override functions without having to modify anything within the component will become very handy. Another great advantage will be defining custom localization configurations directly in the factory. This will guarantee that we have the proper localization wherever we use D3.js in the component.

Moreover, in every component, we use the injected `d3` variable in a private scope of a function and not in the global scope. This is absolutely necessary for clean and encapsulated components; we should never use any variables from global scope within an AngularJS component.

Now, let's create a second module that stores all the visualization-specific code dependent on D3.js. Thus, we want to create an injectable factory for D3.js, as shown in the following code:

```
/* src/chart.js */
// Chart Module

angular.module('myChart', [])

// D3 Factory
.factory('d3', function() {

  /* We could declare locals or other D3.js
     specific configurations here. */

  return d3;
});
```

In the preceding example, we returned d3 without modifying it from the global scope. We can also define custom D3.js specific configurations here (such as locals and formatters). We can go one step further and load the complete D3.js code inside this factory so that d3 will not be available in the global scope at all. However, we don't use this approach here to keep things as simple and understandable as possible.

We need to make this module or parts of it available to the main application. In AngularJS, we can do this by injecting the myChart module into the myApp application as follows:

```
/* src/app.js */

angular.module('myApp', ['myChart']);
```

Usually, we will just inject the directives and services of the visualization module that we want to use in the application, not the whole module. However, for the start and to access all parts of the visualization, we will leave it like this. We can use the components of the chart module now on the AngularJS application by injecting them into the controllers, services, and directives.

The boilerplate—with a simple chart.js and chart.css file—is now ready. We can start to design the chart directive. The chart.spec.js and chart.e2e.js files will be discussed in the last section of this chapter.

A chart directive

Next, we want to create a reusable and testable chart directive. The first question that comes into one's mind is where to put which functionality? Should we create a svg element as parent for the directive or a div element? Should we draw a data point as a circle in svg and use ng-repeat to replicate these points in the chart? Or should we better create and modify all data points with D3.js? I will answer all these question in the following sections.

A directive for SVG

As a general rule, we can say that different concepts should be encapsulated so that they can be replaced anytime by a new technology. Hence, we will use AngularJS with an element directive as a parent element for the visualization. We will bind the data and the options of the chart to the private scope of the directive. In the directive itself, we will create the complete chart including the parent svg container, the axis, and all data points using D3.js.

Let's first add a simple directive for the chart component:

```
/* src/chart.js */
...

// Scatter Chart Directive
.directive('myScatterChart', ["d3",
  function(d3){

    return {
      restrict: 'E',
      scope: {

      },
      compile: function( element, attrs, transclude ) {

        // Create a SVG root element
        var svg = d3.select(element[0]).append('svg');

        // Return the link function
        return function(scope, element, attrs) { };
      }
    };
}]);
```

In the preceding example, we first inject d3 to the directive by passing it as an argument to the caller function. Then, we return a directive as an element with a private scope. Next, we define a custom compile function that returns the link function of the directive. This is important because we need to create the svg container for the visualization during the compilation of the directive. Then, during the link phase of the directive, we need to draw the visualization.

Let's try to define some of these directives and look at the generated output. We define three directives in the index.html file, as shown in the following code:

```
<!-- index.html -->
<div ng-controller="MainCtrl">

  <!-- We can use the visualization directives here -->

  <!-- The first chart -->
  <my-scatter-chart class="chart"></my-scatter-chart>

  <!-- A second chart -->
  <my-scatter-chart class="chart"></my-scatter-chart>
```

```
<!-- Another chart -->
<my-scatter-chart class="chart"></my-scatter-chart>

</div>
```

If we look at the output of the `html` page in the developer tools, we can see that for each base element of the directive, we created a `svg` parent element for the visualization:

```
Q    🗔  │ Elements │ Network  Sources  Timeline  Profiles  Resources  Audits  Console
▼ <html ng-app="myApp" class="ng-scope">
  ▶ <head>…</head>
  ▼ <body>
      <!-- index.html -->
    ▼ <div ng-controller="MainCtrl" class="ng-scope">
        <!-- We can use the visualization directives here -->
        <!-- The first chart -->
      ▼ <my-scatter-chart class="chart ng-isolate-scope">
        ▶ <svg>…</svg>
        </my-scatter-chart>
        <!-- A second chart -->
      ▼ <my-scatter-chart class="chart ng-isolate-scope">
        ▶ <svg>…</svg>
        </my-scatter-chart>
        <!-- Another chart -->
      ▼ <my-scatter-chart class="chart ng-isolate-scope">
        ▶ <svg>…</svg>
        </my-scatter-chart>
      </div>
    </body>
  </html>


html.ng-scope   body   div.ng-scope
```

Output of the HTML page

In the resulting DOM tree, we can see that three `svg` elements are appended to the directives. We can now start to draw the chart in these directives. Let's fill these elements with some awesome charts.

Implementing a custom compile function

First, let's add a data attribute to the isolated scope of the directive. This gives us access to the dataset, which we will later pass to the directive in the HTML template. Next, we extend the compile function of the directive to create a g group container for the data points and the axis. We will also add a watcher that checks for changes of the scope data array. Every time the data changes, we call a draw() function that redraws the chart of the directive. Let's get started:

```
/* src/capp..js */
...
// Scatter Chart Directive
.directive('myScatterChart', ["d3",
  function(d3){

    // we will soon implement this function
    var draw = function(svg, width, height, data){ … };

    return {
      restrict: 'E',
      scope: {
        data: '='
      },
      compile: function( element, attrs, transclude ) {

        // Create a SVG root element
        var svg = d3.select(element[0]).append('svg');

        svg.append('g').attr('class', 'data');
        svg.append('g').attr('class', 'x-axis axis');
        svg.append('g').attr('class', 'y-axis axis');

        // Define the dimensions for the chart
        var width = 600, height = 300;

        // Return the link function
        return function(scope, element, attrs) {

          // Watch the data attribute of the scope
          scope.$watch('data', function(newVal, oldVal, scope) {

            // Update the chart
            draw(svg, width, height, scope.data);
          }, true);
        };
      }
    };
}]);
```

Now, we implement the draw() function in the beginning of the directive.

Drawing charts

So far, the chart directive should look like the following code. We will now implement the `draw()` function, draw axis, and time series data. We start with setting the height and width for the `svg` element as follows:

```
/* src/chart.js */
...

// Scatter Chart Directive
.directive('myScatterChart', ["d3",
  function(d3){

    function draw(svg, width, height, data) {
      svg
        .attr('width', width)
        .attr('height', height);
      // code continues here
    }

    return {
      restrict: 'E',
      scope: {
        data: '='
      },
      compile: function( element, attrs, transclude ) { ... }
    }]);
```

Axis, scale, range, and domain

As you learned in the last chapter, we first need to create the scales for the data and then the axis for the chart. The implementation looks very similar to the scatter chart of the last chapter. We want to update the axis with the minimum and maximum values of the dataset; therefore, we also add this code to the `draw()` function:

```
/* src/chart.js --> myScatterChart --> draw() */

function draw(svg, width, height, data) {
  ...
  // Define a margin
  var margin = 30;

  // Define x-scale
```

```
    var xScale = d3.time.scale()
      .domain([
        d3.min(data, function(d) { return d.time; }),
        d3.max(data, function(d) { return d.time; })
      ])
      .range([margin, width-margin]);

    // Define x-axis
    var xAxis = d3.svg.axis()
      .scale(xScale)
      .orient('top')
      .tickFormat(d3.time.format('%S'));

    // Define y-scale
    var yScale = d3.time.scale()
      .domain([0, d3.max(data, function(d) { return d.visitors; })])
      .range([margin, height-margin]);

    // Define y-axis
    var yAxis = d3.svg.axis()
      .scale(yScale)
      .orient('left')
      .tickFormat(d3.format('f'));

    // Draw x-axis
    svg.select('.x-axis')
      .attr("transform", "translate(0, " + margin + ")")
      .call(xAxis);

    // Draw y-axis
    svg.select('.y-axis')
      .attr("transform", "translate(" + margin + ")")
      .call(yAxis);
  }
```

In the preceding code, we create a timescale for the x-axis and a linear scale for the y-axis and adapt the domain of both axes to match the maximum value of the dataset (we can also use the d3.extent() function to return min and max at the same time). Then, we define the pixel range for our chart area. Next, we create two axes objects with the previously defined scales and specify the tick format of the axis. We want to display the number of seconds that have passed on the x-axis and an integer value of the number of visitors on the y-axis. In the end, we draw the axes by calling the axis generator on the axis selection.

Joining the data points

Now, we will draw the data points and the axis. We finish the `draw()` function with this code:

```
/* src/chart.js --> myScatterChart --> draw() */
function draw(svg, width, height, data) {
    ...
    // Add new the data points
    svg.select('.data')
      .selectAll('circle').data(data)
      .enter()
      .append('circle');

    // Updated all data points
    svg.select('.data')
      .selectAll('circle').data(data)
      .attr('r', 2.5)
      .attr('cx', function(d) { return xScale(d.time); })
      .attr('cy', function(d) { return yScale(d.visitors); });
}
```

In the preceding code, we first create circle elements for the enter join for the data points where no corresponding circle is found in the Selection. Then, we update the attributes of the center point of all circle elements of the chart.

Let's look at the generated output of the application:

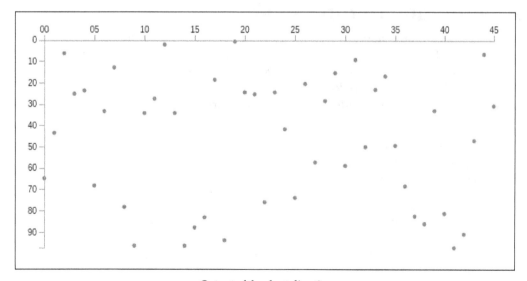

Output of the chart directive

We notice that the axes and the whole chart scales as soon as new data points are added to the chart, similar to the example of the previous chapter. In fact, this result looks very similar to the previous example with the main difference that we used a directive to draw this chart. This means that the data of the visualization that belongs to the application is stored and updated in the application itself, whereas the directive is completely decoupled from the data.

To achieve a nice output like in the previous figure, we need to add some styles to the `cart.css` file, as shown in the following code:

```
/* src/chart.css */
.axis path, .axis line {
    fill: none;
    stroke: #999;
    shape-rendering: crispEdges;
}
.tick {
    font: 10px sans-serif;
}
circle {
    fill: steelblue;
}
```

We need to disable the filling of the axis and enable crisp edges rendering; this will give the whole visualization a much better look.

Advantages of directives

We can see this immediately if we add more directives to the application. Each directive will behave on its own and act in its own scope, whereas the application stores all the data. We can simply add three more charts by extending the `index.html` file and providing more logs data via a `moreLogs` array (defined on the `MainCtrl` and filled with random data for four charts):

```
<!-- index.html -->
<div ng-controller="MainCtrl">
  <my-scatter-chart class="chart" data="moreLogs[0]">
  </my-scatter-chart>
  <my-scatter-chart class="chart" data="moreLogs[1]">
  </my-scatter-chart>
  <my-scatter-chart class="chart" data="moreLogs[2]">
  </my-scatter-chart>
  <my-scatter-chart class="chart" data="moreLogs[3]">
  </my-scatter-chart>
</div>
```

In the generated output, we can now see that four charts are getting filled with the data from the logs:

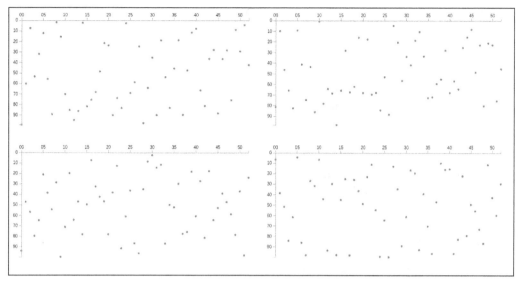

Output of four logs shows four isolated directives

In the preceding output, we can see that now four charts are drawn on the screen. This means that we have successfully implemented the chart directive and are now able to place a `my-scatter-chart` tag in the HTML file and bind the proper data, instead of recalling a JavaScript function to do so. A big advantage of AngularJS and the concept of directives is that we can implement a set of chart directives that can be easily reused by people without a deep knowledge of JavaScript, for example, designers that are much more comfortable writing HTML tags than JavaScript functions (and messing around with the DOM). We also notice that with the use of directives, we are declaring the chart in HTML rather than calling it in JavaScript.

Generalizing the chart directive

The preceding directive works fine for our example and fulfills our goal of a reusable component. However, we explicitly referred to the `time` and `visitors` property of the dataset. It will be much better if the chart directive can display all kinds of datasets, not just those with this specific properties. Therefore, we will create a mapping function, which maps the custom dataset object to a general object, such as {x, y}. The advantage is clear; now, we just have to add a mapping function, and we can immediately display all kinds of different dataset objects, such as {date, errors} or {t, value}. This concept is called generalization.

Let's generalize the `draw()` function as follows:

```
/* src/chart.js --> myScatterChart --> draw() */
function draw(svg, width, height, data) {


   . . .
   // Define x scale
   var xScale = d3.time.scale()
      .domain(d3.extent(data, function(d) { return d.x; }))
      .range([margin, width-margin]);

   // Define y-scale
   var yScale = d3.time.scale()
      .domain([0, d3.max(data, function(d) { return d.y; })])
      .range([margin, height-margin]);


   . . .
   // Updated all data points
   svg.select('.data')
      .selectAll('circle').data(data)
      .attr('r', 2.5)
      .attr('cx', function(d) { return xScale(d.x); })
      .attr('cy', function(d) { return yScale(d.y); });
}
```

Now, we need to add a mapping function to map the dataset to the internal format, as shown in the following code:

```
/* src/chart.js */
. . .
// Scatter Chart Directive
.directive('myScatterChart', ["d3",
   function(d3){

      function draw(svg, width, height, data) { ... }

      return {
         restrict: 'E',
         scope: {
            data: '='
         },
         compile: function( element, attrs, transclude ) {
            . . .

            // Return the link function
```

```
      return function(scope, element, attrs) {

        // Watch the data attribute of the scope
        scope.$watch('data', function(newVal, oldVal, scope) {

          // Map the data to internal format
          var data = scope.data.map(function(d){
            return {
              x: d.time,
              y: d.visitors
            }
          });

          // Update the chart
          draw(svg, width, height, data);
        }, true);

      };
    }
  };
}]);
```

In the preceding code, we simply call the map function on the `data` array and return the internal data point representation of the chart library. Then, instead of the raw `scope.data` array, we call the `draw()` function with this new `data` array.

Testing the directive

Testing is a very important and indispensable technique when writing good quality code. It makes sure that developers can test code repeatedly and automatically, for example, after the code was modified or when it runs in a different environment. Therefore, testing makes your code scalable, maintainable, and hopefully bug free.

Often, tests of a software are also seen as a documentation of the code because the tests show the proper usage of the code with all possible arguments and options. Moreover, this documentation is always up-to-date and executable, which is a huge advantage to static documentations.

In general, there exist multiple levels for software tests:

- **Unit tests**: It is used to test single encapsulated components (functions)
- **Integration tests**: It is used to test the integration of two or more components
- **System tests**: It is used to test the entire application in the complete system stack

When developing frontend JavaScript code, it's common to test the first two levels: unit tests on the local development machine after each file save and integration tests on the testing environment after each committed change. We mostly use so-called test runners to bootstrap, configure a testing environment, and test a framework for an easier and clear testing syntax.

Unit tests are often referred to as **specs** because they are describing and testing the specification of a component. In a test-driven development, we will even write the specs of the component first before implementing it. In AngularJS, we use Karma as the test runner software and Jasmine as the testing framework.

Integration tests are often referred to as **end-to-end (e2e)** because they represent the integration of the component within an application into the web browser. A user action or request in the browser is sent all the way through the application and is responded by the component. The response is tested in the browser. In AngularJS, we use Protractor as the test runner software and Jasmine as the testing framework.

Setting up the testing environment

Before we can start to test the component, we need to set up a testing environment. For the purpose of this book, we will install Karma and Protractor on the local machine and run unit tests as well as integration tests on the local development machine.

Getting started with Karma

Karma is the de facto unit test runner for AngularJS applications and built by the AngularJS team. It takes care of all AngularJS-specific setup and configurations and provides a rich toolset to test AngularJS applications.

Let's install Karma and its command-line interface globally on our machine; to do so, we execute the following command in the root folder of the project:

```
sudo npm install -g karma karma-cli
```

We also want to use Angular-Mocks, a module that supports injecting mocks of AngularJS services into the application; therefore, we install it by running the following command:

```
bower install angular-mocks#1.3.14
```

Now, we can set up a configuration for Karma to run the unit tests; we can use Karma to initialize the configuration. We type the following command in the terminal:

```
karma init test/config/karma.conf.js
```

This will start an interactive prompt, where we can select the settings for the configuration; this dialog box will look similar to the following figure:

```
⊗ ⊙ ⊙   ckoerner@ckoerner-ThinkPad-T430: ~/Dropbox/not-private/Projekte/Interactive Data ∨
Visualizations with AngularJS and D3.js/chapter_4/code$ karma init test/config/k
arma.conf.js

Which testing framework do you want to use ?
Press tab to list possible options. Enter to move to the next question.
> jasmine

Do you want to use Require.js ?
This will add Require.js plugin.
Press tab to list possible options. Enter to move to the next question.
> no

Do you want to capture any browsers automatically ?
Press tab to list possible options. Enter empty string to move to the next quest
ion.
> Chrome
>

What is the location of your source and test files ?
You can use glob patterns, eg. "js/*.js" or "test/**/*Spec.js".
Enter empty string to move to the next question.
> test/spec/**/*.spec.js
>

Should any of the files included by the previous patterns be excluded ?
You can use glob patterns, eg. "**/*.swp".
Enter empty string to move to the next question.
>

Do you want Karma to watch all the files and run the tests on change ?
Press tab to list possible options.
> yes

Config file generated at "/home/ckoerner/Dropbox/not-private/Projekte/Interactiv
e Data Visualizations with AngularJS and D3.js/chapter_4/code/test/config/karma.
conf.js".

ckoerner@ckoerner-ThinkPad-T430:~/Dropbox/not-private/Projekte/Interactive Data
```

Console output when initializing Karma configuration

We will select Jasmine as the testing framework, Chrome as the testing browser, and a pattern to search files like the following `test/spec/**/*.spec.js`. This means that Karma looks for all files in all the subfolders of the `test/spec/` directory to find files with a `.spec.js` ending.

We need to open the previously generated configuration file and edit the `files` section at hand. We extend it to also load AngularJS, Angular-Mocks, and all our application files as follows:

```
/* test/config/karma.conf.js */
// list of files / patterns to load in the browser
  files: [
    'bower_components/angular/angular.js',
```

```
        'bower_components/angular-mocks/angular-mocks.js',
        'bower_components/d3/d3.js',
        'app/src/**/*.js',
        'test/spec/**/*.spec.js'
    ],
```

We defined Chrome as the browser to run the unit tests. On Linux, we need to tell Karma where to find the executable of Chrome. Hence, we export the path to `chromium-browser`, as shown in the following code snippet:

export CHROME_BIN=/usr/bin/chromium-browser

 We can look for the path of the executable of Chrome by typing which `chromium-browser` to the terminal. If we permanently want to export the path of Chrome's binary, we can add the preceding line to the `~/.bashrc` file.

Now, we can start the Karma test runner and keep it opened and running during the development of the visualization component. It will autorun the test suite whenever we save changes to a file.

Getting started with Protractor

Protractor is the de facto standard tool to run integration tests for AngularJS applications and it's built by the AngularJS team. It manages all the AngularJS-specific details (such as scaffolding the application, and so on) for us. Protractor provides an easy API to interact with the AngularJS application in our tests.

Let's install Protractor globally on our machine; this can be achieved by running the following command in the terminal:

sudo npm install -g protractor

When we execute the preceding command, `protractor` and `webdriver-manager` — a manager for the web page testing tool Selenium web driver — command-line tools will be installed. Selenium is a tool to control different browsers from the command line, whereas Protractor is a wrapper for Selenium web driver, which offers AngularJS-specific functionality and settings. Note that Selenium also needs a Java Runtime Environment to be installed.

First, we need to install the latest Selenium binaries. We use the webdriver manager for this and call the update function:

sudo webdriver-manager update

Protractor is using the standard browsers on your machine to access your application. Therefore, we want to make sure that it can access the application without problems. To do so, we will install a very simple static web server (http-server) that serves the application files for Protractor:

```
sudo npm install -g http-server
```

Now, we need to create a configuration for Protractor; we create a `test/config/protractor.conf.js` file with the following content:

```
/* test/config/protractor.conf.js */
exports.config = {

  // The address of a running selenium server.
  seleniumAddress: 'http://localhost:4444/wd/hub',

  // Spec patterns are relative to the configuration file location
  passed
  // to proractor (in this example conf.js).
  // They may include glob patterns.
  specs: [
    '../e2e/**/*.e2e.js'
  ],

  baseUrl: 'http://127.0.0.1:8000',

  // Options to be passed to Jasmine-node.
  jasmineNodeOpts: {
    showColors: true, // Use colors in the command line report.
  }
};
```

 Unlike Karma, we need to define a testing directory that is relative to the configuration file for Protractor!

In the preceding configuration, we tell Protractor to look in the `test/e2e/` folder in all subfolders for files with the `.e2e.js` ending. We also defined `127.0.0.1:8000` as our base URL for the application. Later, we need to make sure that http-server is serving the application at port `8000`.

Unit testing the chart directive

We need to check every unit of the software on its own for its proper usage. Let's unit test the chart component with the Karma test runner and Jasmine as a testing framework. We want to automatically check whether the chart directive creates the correct elements, nodes, and draws the correct circles when data is assigned to it. We open the `chart.spec.js` file in the `test/spec/` directory and start with creating a test suite for the directive, as shown in the following code:

```
/* test/spec/chart.spec.js */
describe('my-scatter-chart', function() {
  /* Here goes the code for the test suite */

});
```

We open the terminal in the root directory of the project and let Karma autowatch the file changes and run the test suite as follows:

karma start test/config/karma.conf.js

We see that the test finishes with errors because we have not defined any tests yet; the output should look similar to the following figure:

Output of running the empty test suite with Karma

We need to configure and initialize the module and the directive in test suite before running each test; this can be done easily with the `beforeEach()` function. Let's add some bootstrapping code for the tests:

```
/* test/spec/chart.spec.js */
var elm, scope;

beforeEach(module('myChart'));

beforeEach(inject(function($rootScope, $compile) {

    /* Define the Directive */
    elm = angular.element(
```

```
    '<my-scatter-chart class="chart" data="data">' +
    '</my-scatter-chart>');

    /* Define the Data on the Scope */
    scope = $rootScope.$new();
    scope.data = [];

    $compile(elm)(scope);
    scope.$digest();
}));
```

In the preceding code, we can see that before each test specification, we will initialize the myChart module and compile a directive with sample data on its scope, that is, $rootScope.$new(). This creates a new isolated scope for the directive.

 You can find more detailed information on Karma on the projects website at http://karma-runner.github.io/.

Now, we can run the first real test; we want to check whether the svg parent element is created for the directive. We first create a test specification and then check whether the number of svg elements in the directive equals to 1:

```
/* test/spec/chart.spec.js */
it('should create svg parent', function() {
    var svg = elm.find('svg');
    expect(svg.length).toBe(1);
});
```

The syntax of the Jasmine testing framework is written in an understandable way and should read easily like a short description of the test.

 Read the introduction to Jasmine on its web page at http://jasmine.github.io/2.0/introduction.html, if the syntax is not completely clear.

When we switch back to the terminal, we should see that Karma has restarted the test suite and already shows the result—this time our tests are passing, great.

```
ckoerner@ckoerner-ThinkPad-T430: ~/Dropbox/not-private/Projekte/Interactive Data Visualizations with AngularJS and D3.js/chapter

ckoerner@ckoerner-ThinkPad-T430: ~/Dropbox/not-private/Projekte/In...  ×   ckoerner@ckoerner-ThinkPad-T430: ~/Dropbox/not-private/Projekte/In...  ×

ckoerner@ckoerner-ThinkPad-T430:~/Dropbox/not-private/Projekte/Interactive Data Visualizations with AngularJS and D3.
js/chapter_4/code$ karma start test/config/karma.conf.js
INFO [karma]: Karma v0.12.24 server started at http://localhost:9876/
INFO [launcher]: Starting browser Chrome
INFO [Chromium 34.0.1847 (Ubuntu)]: Connected on socket ytUb6pkQhsVqBzp1-J9a with id 96583138
Chromium 34.0.1847 (Ubuntu): Executed 0 of 0 ERROR (0.011 secs / 0 secs)
INFO [watcher]: Changed file "/home/ckoerner/Dropbox/not-private/Projekte/Interactive Data Visualizations with Angula
rJS and D3.js/chapter_4/code/test/spec/chart.spec.js".
Chromium 34.0.1847 (Ubuntu): Executed 3 of 3 SUCCESS (0.115 secs / 0.112 secs)
INFO [watcher]: Changed file "/home/ckoerner/Dropbox/not-private/Projekte/Interactive Data Visualizations with Angula
rJS and D3.js/chapter_4/code/test/spec/chart.spec.js".
Chromium 34.0.1847 (Ubuntu): Executed 3 of 3 SUCCESS (0.135 secs / 0.127 secs)
INFO [watcher]: Changed file "/home/ckoerner/Dropbox/not-private/Projekte/Interactive Data Visualizations with Angula
rJS and D3.js/chapter_4/code/test/spec/chart.spec.js".
Chromium 34.0.1847 (Ubuntu): Executed 3 of 3 SUCCESS (0.094 secs / 0.083 secs)
```

Karma runs the tests automatically in the background

Now, we can continue and also test the group container elements, which contain the data points and the axis. We add the following specification:

```
/* test/spec/chart.spec.js */
it('should create containers for data and axis', function() {
    var groups = elm.find('svg').find('g');
    expect(groups.length).toBe(3);
});
```

We also see that this test will autorun and pass. Now, we can go one step further and simulate a change on the scope data so that the directive can update and draw some data points. We add another specification:

```
/* test/spec/chart.spec.js */
it('should create a data point', function() {
    var circles = elm.find('svg').find('circle');
    expect(circles.length).toBe(0);

    scope.data.push({
      time: (new Date('2014-01-01 00:00:00')).toString(),
      visitors:3
    });
    scope.$digest();

    circles = elm.find('svg').find('circle');
    expect(circles.length).toBe(1);
});
```

In the preceding code, it's observed that we can easily modify the scope and trigger a digest cycle by calling `scope.$digest()`. Now, we can go into more details, add different data points, and check whether they are set properly. In general, one should test all possible combinations of the input data for a component under test.

E2E testing of the chart directive

We want to create the integration tests of the chart directive and test the proper behavior of the chart directive if a user interacts with the visualization. In integration tests, the visualization component is integrated in the application and tested together with the application. Unfortunately, we have not implemented any form of interaction yet. Therefore, we will just initialize the testing setup for our component and develop integration tests later in this book.

Let's create e2e tests for the chart directive with the Protractor test runner and Jasmine as a testing framework. We create a simple test suite in the `chart.spec.js` file in the `test/e2e/` folder:

```
/* test/e2e/chart.e2e.js */
describe('Scatter Chart application', function() {
  /* Here goes the code for the test suite */

});
```

Usually, we will not run these tests on the local machine on every file save, but more likely on a testing environment on every committed change in the version control. For now, we will just run everything on the development machine. First, we need to start the webdriver with the following command:

webdriver-manager start

Next, we serve the application files with the http-server tool in a new terminal window as follows:

http-server -p 8000

We switch again to a new terminal and call Protractor with the following configuration file:

protractor test/config/protractor.conf.js

This starts the test runner who checks the files that are matching the pattern defined in the configuration file and runs the tests on them.

```
ckoerner@ckoerner-ThinkPad-T430: ~/Dropbox/not-private/Projekte/Interactive Data Visualizations with AngularJS and D3.js/chapter
ckoerner@ckoerner-ThinkPad-T430: ~/Dropbox/not-private/Projekte/In...  ×   ckoerner@ckoerner-ThinkPad-T430: ~/Dropbox/not-private/Projekte/In...  ×
ckoerner@ckoerner-ThinkPad-T430:~/Dropbox/not-private/Projekte/Interactive Data Visualizations with AngularJS and D3.
js/chapter_4/code$ protractor test/config/protractor.conf.js
Using the selenium server at http://localhost:4444/wd/hub


Finished in 0.007 seconds
0 tests, 0 assertions, 0 failures

ckoerner@ckoerner-ThinkPad-T430:~/Dropbox/not-private/Projekte/Interactive Data Visualizations with AngularJS and D3.
js/chapter_4/code$ █
```

Protractor output for a blank test suite

In the preceding screenshot, we see the output when running protractor on our project—the empty test suite. Unlike Karma, Protractor returns no error for an empty test suite. We also remark that we have to start the test manually every time we want to use it.

 You can find more information on Protractor scenario runner on its home page at http://angular.github.io/ protractor/.

Let's create a simple test where we test the previously developed page that displays four scatter charts if all four svg gets successfully created. First, we initialize a beforeEach() function that executes code before every test. We want to load the content from the index.html file here and then write a test to check whether the application contains four charts:

```
describe('Scatter Chart application', function() {

    beforeEach(function() {
        browser.get('index.html');
    });

    it('has 4 charts', function() {

      var charts = element.all(by.css('svg'));
      expect(charts.count()).toEqual(4);
    });
});
```

We run Protractor again and hopefully also pass this test. Now, we are prepared for developing more exciting features!

Summary

In this chapter, you learned how to properly integrate a D3.js component into an AngularJS application — the *Angular* way. All files, modules, and components should be maintainable, testable, and reusable.

You learned how to set up an AngularJS application and how to structure the folder structure for the visualization component. We put different responsibilities in different files and modules. Every piece that we can separate from the main application can be reused in another application; the goal is to use as much modularization as possible.

As a next step, we created the visualization directive by implementing a custom compile function. This gives us access to the first compilation of the element — where we can append the svg element as a parent for the visualization — and other container elements.

Then, we discussed the setup of testing frameworks in AngularJS. We used the Karma test runner to test different separate units and the Protractor test runner to test the integration of the component in the browser and the users' interaction.

In the next chapter, you will learn how to load and parse data with D3.js and how to integrate these functionalities into the AngularJS world. We will use this knowledge to load, parse, and display real-world data in our visualization.

5
Loading and Parsing Data

In the previous chapters, you learned how to create a simple scatter chart directive with D3.js and include it in an AngularJS application. Until now, we just generated random data to plot in charts.

In this chapter, you will learn how to feed the visualization directive with real data. Therefore, we need to load raw data from an external resource, we need to parse it to JavaScript objects, and we need to group the data for the visualization. First, we need to load log files from a remote server. Therefore, we will take a look at different techniques to load data into the AngularJS application: *XHR* with D3.js and *$http* with AngularJS. The goal is to understand the advantages and disadvantages of these techniques and to know which data loading module suits the best for the visualization application.

Once we have the raw data in the format of a string on the client, we need to parse and process it in order to feed it into the JavaScript application. This means parsing the log string into an array of readable and debugable objects and grouping the log data in nice intervals. We rather want to display the number of errors in a certain interval (for example, 1 minute) than plotting every single error log in the chart. In the following section, you will learn how to build a flexible *parser* service to generate a JavaScript object out of a string of data logs. We will also build a very simple *Classifier* to group the logs in intervals and display aggregated information. In this chapter you will learn how to:

- Load data from external resources
- Choose the best XHR wrapper for your application
- Parse log strings into JavaScript objects
- Group data to display aggregated information
- Plot real data from a log file

Loading external data

In a modern web application, it's a common task to load and reload data from external resources, regardless of whether we read from the database or plain text files. Thus, nearly every JavaScript framework includes its own functions to load external data, that is, in most of the cases a wrapper of the native XMLHttpRequest (XHR) object. In our application setup, we have the following options to load external data:

- XMLHttpRequest: This is a native XHR object provided by most modern browsers
- d3.xhr(): This is a wrapper function for the XMLHttpRequest object in D3.js
- $http: This is an Angular wrapper module for the XMLHttpRequest object

These implementations use the unidirectional XMLHttpRequest to request data from a web server. Unidirectional means that we can solely request data from the client and then wait for the response of the server. Thus, we also don't know if there is *new* data available on the server. If we want a "real-time-like" behavior, we will need to continuously send requests.

Real real-time behavior needs a real bidirectional connection instead of an unidirectional request. WebSockets provide such a bidirectional connection over TCP for modern web browsers. This means that the client is connected with the server and data changes can be pushed from the server directly to the client — rather than requesting them. In this chapter, we will look at d3.xhr() and $http in more detail. In the last chapter, we will use WebSockets and the socket.io library to push changes in real time to the client.

Let's get started and take a look at a real Apache access log file:

```
test/access.log.66.249.64.121 - - [22/Nov/2014:01:56:00 +0100]
  "GET /index.html HTTP/1.1" 200 2507 "-" "Mozilla/5.0 (X11; Linux
  x86_64) AppleWebKit/537.36 (KHTML, like Gecko) Ubuntu
  Chromium/41.0.2272.76 Chrome/41.0.2272.76 Safari/537.36"
66.249.64.129 - - [22/Nov/2014:01:56:01 +0100] "GET / HTTP/1.1"
  200 2487 "-" "Mozilla/5.0 (X11; Linux x86_64) AppleWebKit/537.36
  (KHTML, like Gecko) Ubuntu Chromium/41.0.2272.76
  Chrome/41.0.2272.76 Safari/537.36"
66.249.64.125 - - [22/Nov/2014:03:09:07 +0100] "GET /about.html
  HTTP/1.1" 200 2525 "-" "Mozilla/5.0 (X11; Linux x86_64)
  AppleWebKit/537.36 (KHTML, like Gecko) Ubuntu
  Chromium/41.0.2272.76 Chrome/41.0.2272.76 Safari/537.36"
```

First, we want to load this file with our application. To not raise any *cross origin request* errors in our local browser, we have to again use a static web server. We can do this by starting `http-server` in the root directory of our project:

```
http-server -p 8000
```

Now, we will navigate to `http://localhost:8000/files/access.log` in the browser and see the full content of the log file (see the following screenshot). Perfect! Now, we will try to load this file in JavaScript.

Viewing the log file in the browser

XHR – the native XMLHttpRequest

`XMLHttpRequest` (XHR) is a native interface that implements HTTP requests in JavaScript; therefore it represents the foundation of the *AJAX* technology and is available in most modern browsers.

AJAX is an acronym for **Asynchronous JavaScript And XML**. It stands for requesting the XML data from within JavaScript. However, nowadays, we use the much simpler and more accessible JSON format instead of XML. To understand the following abstractions and wrappers of XHR, we want to first see and understand the native XHR object. Here is a very simple example:

```
var url = "files/access.log";
var r = new XMLHttpRequest();
r.open("GET", url, true);
r.onreadystatechange = function() {
```

```
    if (r.readyState != 4 || r.status != 200) return;
    console.log(r.responseText);
};
r.send();
```

In the preceding code, we first generated an `XMLHttpRequest` object and used the `.open()` function to load a specific file. Then, we added a callback function, which is executed on the `onreadystatechange` event. To trigger this event and to execute the callback function, we need to send the request by calling the `.send()` method on the `XMLHttpRequest` object. When the server responds to the client, the `onreadystatechange` event gets triggered. Once the response is complete, the `readyState` parameter on the response object will be set to the status code `4`. If the server responds with a status `200 (OK)`, we print the body of the response. The output of the request will look similar to the following screenshot:

Output of the XHR request using the native `XMLHttpRequest`

For more information and detailed documentation of the methods and events of the `XMLHttpRequest` object, visit https://developer.mozilla.org/en-US/docs/Web/API/XMLHttpRequest.

The implementation does not look very difficult and is straightforward. Nevertheless, it requires a lot of code to call a simple GET request with XHR. We can easily write this code in our application and it will work for us, but we will not do it because we forgot an important point with this implementation. It's the *native* XHR implementation of the browser. Therefore, like every native implementation, its behavior is not the same across different browsers. To avoid dealing with cross-browser issues and to have an easier syntax, we will continue using the XHR wrapper of D3.js.

d3.xhr – the XHR wrapper of D3.js

D3.js provides the `d3.xhr(url[, mimeType] [, callback])` method, which is a useful and easy-to-use wrapper on the `XMLHttpRequest` object. As a callback function, we can use a `function(response){}` structure. Let's take a look at the same GET request as before using this method:

```
var url = "files/access.log";
var xhr = d3.xhr(url, function(response){
  console.log(response.responseText);
});
```

Wow! This API is much simpler than before and the output looks exactly the same (see the following screenshot):

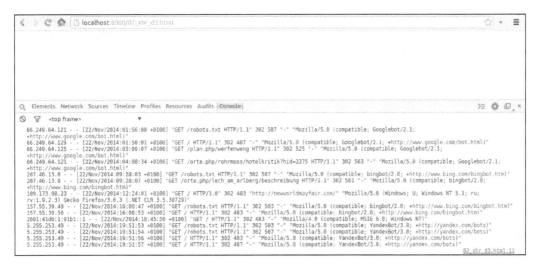

Output of the XHR request using d3.xhr()

At the top, D3.js implements more useful methods such as `.get([callback])` and `.post([data] [, callback])` on the `xhr` object . Let's take a look at two examples that return the same list of logs as before:

```
var url = "files/access.log";
var xhr = d3.xhr(url)
  .get(function(error, response){
    console.log(response.responseText);
  });
```

The preceding code implements a GET request, whereas the following code uses a POST request to send additional data to the server:

```
var url = "files/access.log";
var data = {'test': 'my-data'};
var xhr = d3.xhr('url')
  .post(data, function(error, response){
    console.log(response.responseText);
  });
```

In the preceding examples, we saw that the wrappers on the GET and POST requests use a callback function with the `function(error, response){}` structure.

Useful wrappers for common file types

D3.js also implements wrappers for predefined file types. It sets their mime types in the `accept` property of the HTTP header properly and parses the output for us. We can use these functions to load and parse the following data types:

- Plain text: `d3.text(url [, mimeType] [, callback])`
- JSON: `d3.json(url [, callback])`
- XML: `d3.xml(url [, mimeType] [, callback])`
- HTML: `d3.html(url [, callback])`
- CSV (comma-separated): `d3.csv(url [, accessor] [, callback])`
- TSV (tabulation-separated): `d3.tsv(url [, accessor] [, callback])`

In our sample project, we will deal with log files that usually don't have a predefined structure. Therefore, we will use the `d3.text()` function for now. We will write a custom parser for the Apache access logs in the next section.

Creating a simple D3 data loading component

Once we know how to load the external data, we need to include a data loading component to the AngularJS application. The best Angular method to use is to wrap the loader function in a reusable *factory* component. This encapsulates the data loading component and makes it modular, reusable, and testable. Let's implement a service for the data loader for the example application of the previous chapter:

```
/*.src/chart.js.*/
...
// D3 Loader service
.factory('SimpleD3Loader', ["d3",
  function(d3) {
    return function(url, callback) {
      d3.text(url, 'text/plain', callback);
    };
}])
```

The preceding code will create an injectable `SimpleD3Loader` service in the chart module with two arguments called `url` and `callback`. We can now initialize the `d3.text()` function or create a progress listener. The component itself is injectable, reusable, testable, and replaceable—everything that we initially aimed for. Now, we want to use this function to load the data into the AngularJS application. Therefore, we change the main controller of the application to load the data of the log file as follows:

```
/* src/app.js */
// Application Module
angular.module('myApp', ['myChart'])
// Main application controller
.controller('MainCtrl', ["$scope", "SimpleD3Loader", function
  ($scope, SimpleD3Loader) {

  $scope.log = {
    src: 'files/access.log',
    data: ''
  };
  SimpleD3Loader($scope.log.src, function(data){
    $scope.log.data = data;
    $scope.$digest();
  });
}]);
```

In the preceding code of the application module, we inject the `SimpleD3Loader` service into the `MainCtrl` controller. Then, we define a log object and load the `access.log` file with the `SimpleD3Loader` service. We need to add a `$scope.$digest()` call to trigger the digest circle of the controller and inform Angular JS about the changes on the scope. In the following HTML directive, we can now display the content of the log file and see whether the component works:

```
<!-- index.html -->
<div ng-controller="MainCtrl">
  <h3>{{ log.src }}</h3>
  <p>{{ log.data }}</p>
</div>
```

If we look at the resulting HTML page (see the following figure), we see that the log file was successfully loaded and is now available inside the application controller:

Implementing and testing a D3 loading service

Now, we manually tested the component and it looks fine. However, before we continue parsing the log data, we want to make sure that the components always work. Thus, we implement an unit test for the `SimpleD3Loader` service.

Testing the simple D3 data loading component

First, we create a `files/` directory for all the test files inside the test folder. The folder structure should look like this:

- `test/`
- `test/config/`
- `test/e2e/`
- `test/spec/`
- `test/files/`

Now, we add a `testAccessApache.log` file with the following content to the `test/files/` folder:

```
66.249.64.121 - - [22/Nov/2014:01:56:00 +0100] "GET /index.html
   HTTP/1.1" 200 2507 "-" "Mozilla/5.0 (X11; Linux x86_64)
   AppleWebKit/537.36 (KHTML, like Gecko) Ubuntu
   Chromium/41.0.2272.76 Chrome/41.0.2272.76 Safari/537.36"
```

We need to be careful and not add additional line breaks at the end because we want to test the result of the loader against the content of this file.

Let's tell *Karma* that we want to access the files from the `test/files/` folder inside our tests. Therefore, we add the last line of the following snippet to the file pattern list in `test/conf/karma.conf.js`:

```
/* test/conf/karma.conf.js */
...
// list of files / patterns to load in the browser
files: [
  'bower_components/angular/angular.js',
  'bower_components/angular-mocks/angular-mocks.js',
  'bower_components/d3/d3.js',
  'src/**/*.js',
  'test/spec/**/*.spec.js',
  {pattern: 'test/files/**', included: false}
], ...
```

The preceding configuration tells Karma to serve all the files from the `test/files/` directory, but not include them with a `<script>` tag in the generated HTML test file. Finally, we can add the D3 loader test scenario to the previously created data loading service:

```
/* test/spec/chart.spec.js */
describe('simple-d3-loader', function() {
  var elm, scope, loader;
```

```
   beforeEach(module('myChart'));

   beforeEach(inject(function(SimpleD3Loader) {
     loader = SimpleD3Loader;
   })));
});
```

In the preceding code, we see that for each test case, we inject the `SimpleD3Loader` object as a `loader` variable. This means that we can now add an asynchronous test case to test the data loading service. To debug, we can write `iit` instead of `it` to solely run a single test and skip all other tests of the application. However, this requires Jasmine 1.3 and won't work in the current version of Jasmine 2.0.

First, we will create a regular expression to test the access log string against this expression and put it at the beginning of the file.

If you wonder how to create such a regular expression, first take a look at the syntax for regular expression and then use a tool like the one from `https://regex101.com/` to develop and evaluate the expression.

Let's develop a regular expression that matches the access log format:

```
/* test/spec/chart.spec.js */
var accessApacheRegExp = /^([0-9]{0,3}\.[0-9]{0,3}\.[0-
9]{0,3}\.[0-9]{0,3})\s*-(.*?)-\s*\[(.*?)\]\s*"(.*?)"(.*?)\s*"-
"\s*"(.*?)"$/ig;
```

Now, we can add a test to the D3.js Loader scenario.

```
/* test/spec/chart.spec.js    */
it('should load the data', function() {
  var result;
  runs(function() {
    loader('/base/test/files/testAccessApache.log', function
        (error, data){
      result = data;
    });
  });
  waitsFor(function(){
    return result;
  }, "AJAX should complete", 2000);
  runs(function() {
    expect(result).toMatch(accessApacheRegExp);
  });
});
```

The preceding code doesn't look straightforward because we are testing an asynchronous function call (loading the file with XHR is asynchronous). Let's walk through the code step by step.

First, we define a `result` variable that stores the result of the service. Then, we execute the asynchronous function using a first `runs()` block until the following `waitsFor()` block returns `true`. We observe that this block takes a time-out value as a third argument that stops the run block after the time-out is reached. In the second `runs()` block, which is executed after the first one has stopped, we implement the `expect()` statement to check the actual `result`.

 Once you understand the `runs-waitFor-runs` order, it should not be hard to write asynchronous tests yourself. Bear in mind that we can also mock the behavior of the asynchronous function to behave synchronously. We will see this in the following section.

Now, we can run the test by starting Karma with the following command:

```
karma start test/config/karma.conf.js
```

When we check the output of Karma, it should run one test successfully and skip the other three tests:

```
ckoerner@ckoerner-ThinkPad-T430: ~/Dropbox/not-private/Projekte/Interactive Data Visualizations with AngularJS an

ckoerner@ckoerner-ThinkPad-T430: ~/Dropbox/not-private/Pr...  ×   ckoerner@ckoerner-ThinkPad-T430: ~/Dropbox/not-private/Pr...  ×

ckoerner@ckoerner-ThinkPad-T430:~/Dropbox/not-private/Projekte/Interactive Data Visualizations with Angul
arJS and D3.js/chapter_5/code$ karma start test/config/karma.conf.js
INFO [karma]: Karma v0.12.24 server started at http://localhost:9876/
INFO [launcher]: Starting browser Chrome
INFO [Chromium 34.0.1847 (Ubuntu)]: Connected on socket BCLz2Yzs4AVAZYBGT7GN with id 3388502
Chromium 34.0.1847 (Ubuntu): Executed 1 of 4 (skipped 3) SUCCESS (0.04 secs / 0.035 secs)
```

Output of the Karma test runner

Cool! We now know that we can work on the code without breaking the functionalities of the existing components.

Summary of D3.js as a data loading service

In this section, you learned how to implement a simple loading component in D3.js and include it as a service in the AngularJS application. We observed that we need to write asynchronous tests to test the service. An obvious advantage would be that if we already have a chart component written in D3.js, we can use this technique to seamlessly integrate it into our application. Also, we can encapsulate the different components and make them reusable and testable.

A reasonable disadvantage is that we have to nest a `draw()` function inside the callback function of the data load function because the data is only available when the callback function is executed. However, we would have to implement event handlers or trigger a digest circle to inform the application about the new data.

If we write the visualization component for the AngularJS application from scratch, we will probably use the AngularJS-specific feature such as the `$http` module, which informs the application about new data for us.

$http – the Angular wrapper for XHR

If we are developing a component for AngularJS, then we should use all the benefits and advantages that this framework provides, such as Promises, caching, mocking, and so on. For XHR, AngularJS provides an easy-to-use function that implements Promises. Let's take a look at an example:

```
var url = "files/access.log";
$http.get(url)
.then(function(response){
  console.log(response.data);
});
```

Looks pretty neat, doesn't it? This is exactly why we want to use an abstraction provided by AngularJS. Now, we can make an HTTP request with all the advantages from the AngularJS world. For completeness, let's also look at the POST request:

```
var url = "files/access.log";
var data = {'test': 'my-data'};
$http.post(url, data)
.then(function(response){
  console.log(response.data);
});
```

Also, the preceding code will load the log file and print it as the previous examples.

Creating an AngularJS data loading component

Now, we will use the AngularJS implementation for the data loading service in our chart module and see the differences to the D3 version. Let's add a new service called `SimpleHttpLoader` and inject the `$http` module:

```
/* src/chart.js */
...
// Simple Http loader service
.factory('SimpleHttpLoader', ["$http",
function($http) {
  return function(url) {
    return $http.get(url);
  }
}])
```

In the preceding code, we wrap the XHR GET requests and return the Promise created by the `$http.get()` method. Now, in the application module, we can replace the `SimpleD3Loader` service with the new `SimpleHttpLoader` service:

```
/* src/app.js */
// Application Module
angular.module('myApp', ['myChart'])
// Main application controller
.controller('MainCtrl', ["$scope", "SimpleHttpLoader",
function ($scope, SimpleHttpLoader) {
  $scope.log = {
    src: 'files/access.log',
    data: ''
  };
  SimpleHttpLoader($scope.log.src)
  .then(function(response){
    $scope.log.data = response.data;
  });
}]);
```

If we run the preceding example, we will see no difference in the resulting output to the previous example. However, we observe that we don't have to trigger the digest circle anymore because the `$http` module does this internally for us.

There are more advantages that are not immediately obvious. Now, we have all the capabilities of the AngularJS `$http` module. This means that we can simply extend the `get` method to `$http.get(url, { cache: true })` and enable caching. Another advantage is that we can use a mock-up of the `$http` module for testing purposes, where the `.get()` method will return the predefined file content directly for a defined URL. This means that in our test scenario, we will not have to wait for the XHR request in every test, but the `.get()` method will return the file content directly.

Testing the AngularJS data loading component

Now, let's create a test for the new service. We need to add a new test scenario, where we set up the mock-up for the $http module called the $httpBackend mock. This allows you to not only perform the real XHR requests every time we run the tests, but it also allows you to respond on a certain route with a predefined result:

```
/* test/spec/chart.spec.js */
...
describe('simple-angular-loader', function() {
  var elm, scope, loader, httpBackend;
  beforeEach(module('myChart'));
  beforeEach(inject(function(SimpleHttpLoader, $httpBackend) {
    loader = SimpleHttpLoader;
    $httpBackend
    .when('GET', '/base/test/files/testAccessApache.log')
    .respond('66.249.64.121 - - [22/Nov/2014:01:56:00 +0100] "GET
    /index.html HTTP/1.1" 200 2507 "-" ""');
    httpBackend = $httpBackend;
  }));
});
```

First, we inject the $httpBackend mock and assign a default response for the route that leads to the log file. Now, we can use the httpBackend mock in our tests instead of loading the test files. Let's implement a test:

```
/* test/spec/chart.spec.js  */
...
it('should load the data', function() {
  var result;
  loader('/base/test/files/testAccessApache.log').then
    (function(response){
    result = response.data;
  });
  httpBackend.flush();
  expect(result).toMatch(accessApacheRegExp);
});
```

In the preceding code, we defined the expected response for the /base/test/files/ testAccessApache.log route to be the content of the file. We should not forget to flush the httpBackend mock-up after the service has called the external resource to tell the $http module to load the results from the $httpBackend mock. It's easy to see that with this technique, we don't need to use the asynchronous test constructs, which we used in the SimpleD3Loader service in our previous example.

Output of the Karma test runner

Summary of AngularJS as a data loading service

If we are writing the data loading component from scratch, we should implement all data loading methods with AngularJS. This enables us to use all the beautiful aspects of AngularJS, such as Promises, mocks, synchronous testing, caching, and so on. Caching requests is performed by simply adding the cache option to the `.get()` function and the mocking of the `$http` module allows you to write synchronous tests with the `$httpBackend` mock.

Parsing log files to JavaScript objects

Once we load the string of log entries, we need to parse these entries to an array of data points in order to display them. We want to parse the plain text log file to an array of JavaScript objects.

In this section, I will show you a convenient way to mix all techniques and to retrieve the best of both worlds. We will implement a preprocessing service component. This uses regular expressions to split the text into an array and D3.js to parse time strings to dates.

Parsing log files step by step

Let's look at the structure of the log files again:

```
66.249.64.121 - - [22/Nov/2014:01:56:00 +0100] "GET /robots.txt
    HTTP/1.1" 302
507 "-" "Mozilla/5.0 (compatible; Googlebot/2.1;
+http://www.google.com/bot.html)"
66.249.64.129 - - [22/Nov/2014:01:56:01 +0100] "GET / HTTP/1.1"
    302 487 "-"
"Mozilla/5.0 (compatible; Googlebot/2.1; +http://www.google.com
    /bot.html)"
```

From this string, we ultimately want to generate an array of JavaScript objects in the shape of [{ip: 66.249.64.121, time: 2014-11-22 01:56:00 +0100, …}, …] as a clean input dataset for the visualization. This means that we first need to cut the string into an array, where each element contains a row of the log file. To remove blank lines and line breaks from the beginning and the end, we should also trim the string. In the following examples, we assume that the data variable contains the string of the log entries. We can use the .split(separator) function to split a string into an array of pieces. Let's try this:

```
var lines = data.trim().split("\n");
console.log(lines);
```

The resulting array looks like this:

Output of splitting text into lines

Now, we need to look at every line and split it into smaller chunks, such as the IP address, the date, and so on. We can see that the - and " symbols could be possible separators; let's split every line using these symbols. We will use the `map()` function on the array of lines to access every line and split it with the `/[-"]/gi` regular expression (this means that we split every line at every occurrence of the - or " symbol):

```
var lines = data.trim().split("\n")
.map(function(line){
  return line.split(/[-"]/gi);
});
console.log(lines);
```

Let's look at the result:

Output of splitting each line

In the output, we can see that we should trim every element in the line and remove the [and] symbols to extract the time properly. We can again use `map()` to process all the elements of a single line. We remove symbols by calling the `replace()` function with the `/["\[\]]/gi` regular expression:

```
var lines = data.trim().split("\n")
.map(function(line){
  return line.split(/[-"]/gi)
  .map(function(element){
    return element.trim().replace(/["\[\]]/gi,'');
  });
});
console.log(lines);
```

Let's take a look at the result:

Output of trimming every word

Now, we extracted the JavaScript array from the log string.

Parsing the custom date format to a JavaScript date

As a next step, we need to parse the date string to JavaScript dates in order to use them in our chart directive. Therefore, we look at the date string provided in log files:

```
22/Nov/2014:01:56:00 +0100
```

We will use D3.js' powerful date formatter to parse the date string to a JavaScript date. To start, we need to define a formatter that has the same format as the string that we want to parse. Thus, we construct a formatter that matches our date:

```
var format = d3.time.format("%d/%b/%Y:%H:%M:%S %Z");
```

Finally, we can also convert the array to an object, which makes it easier to access and use in the visualization process. Again, we map the array and assign the elements to associative keys:

```
var data = r.responseText;
var lines = data.trim().split("\n")
.map(function(line){
  return line.split(/[-"]/gi)
  .map(function(element){
    return element.trim().replace(/["\[\]]/gi,'');
```

```
    });
  });
  var format = d3.time.format("%d/%b/%Y:%H:%M:%S %Z");
  lines = lines.map(function(d){
    return {
      ip: d[0],
      time: format.parse(d[2]),
      request: d[3],
      status: d[4],
      agent: d[8]
    };
  });
  console.log(lines);
```

The resulting array now looks pretty good, as shown in the following screenshot. We parsed the whole log string with a few simple operations to a fully iterable and plotable JavaScript object:

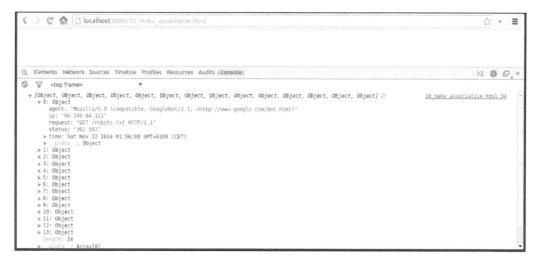

Output of an associative array with parsed dates

A reusable data parsing service

Finally, we will wrap the code to a `StringParser` service and add it to the visualization module and make it injectable, reusable, and testable:

```
/* src/chart.js */
...
// Parser service
.factory('StringParser', function(){
  return function(str, line, word, rem) {
    line = line || "\n";
```

```
        word = word || /[-"]/gi;
        rem = rem || /["\[\]]/gi;

        return str.trim().split(line).map(function(l){
          return l.split(word).map(function(w){
            return w.trim().replace(rem,'');
          });
        });
      };
    })
```

In the preceding code, we create a customizable parser component with the function that we previously developed. Now, we have some basic functionalities to parse a variety of different log strings. Let's see an example where we use the StringParser service in action. We will now parse the log string in the MainCtrl controller of the application module:

```
/* src/app.js */
// Application Module
angular.module('myApp', ['myChart'])
// Main application controller
.controller('MainCtrl', ["$scope", "SimpleHttpLoader",
  "StringParser",
  function ($scope, SimpleHttpLoader, StringParser) {

  var formatter = d3.time.format("%d/%b/%Y:%H:%M:%S %Z");
  $scope.log = {
    src: 'files/access.log',
    data: ''
  };
  SimpleHttpLoader($scope.log.src)
  .then(function(response){
    // Response
    var responseDataStr = response.data;
    // Parse string to an array of datum arrays
    var parsed = StringParser(responseDataStr);
    // Map each datum array to object
    var mapped = parsed.map(function(d) {
      return {
        time: formatter.parse(d[2]),
        ip: d[0],
        request: d[3],
        status: d[4],
        agent: d[8]
      };
    });
    $scope.log.data = mapped;
  });
}]);
```

In the preceding code, we added the previous processing steps to the main controller of the application module. After loading the data, we parse it to an array of arrays and then map it to an array of objects. Now, we can easily access the properties in the template as follows:

```
<!-- index.hmtl -->
<div ng-controller="MainCtrl">
  <h3>{{ log.src }}</h3>
  <div ng-repeat="l in log.data">
    <span>Date: {{ l.time }}</span>
    <span>IP: {{ l.ip }}</span>
    <span>Request: {{ l.request }}</span>
    <hr>
  </div>
</div>
```

The result of the previous template is shown in the following screenshot:

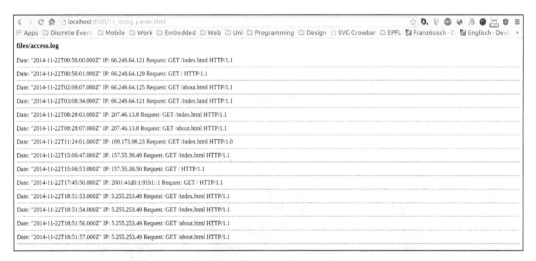

Output of the parsed log entries

Testing the data parsing service

As a last step, we want to write unit tests for the new service. We create a new test scenario for the service and a test case to parse all the values properly:

```
/* test/spec/chart.spec.js */
  var elm, scope, parser, logString;
  beforeEach(module('myChart'));

  beforeEach(inject(function(StringParser) {
```

```
    parser = StringParser;
    logString = '66.249.64.121 - - [22/Nov/2014:01:56:00 +0100]
      "GET /robots.txt HTTP/1.1" 302 507 "-" "Mozilla/5.0
      (compatible; Googlebot/2.1; +http://www.google.com
      /bot.html)"';
  }));
  it('should parse the data', function() {
    var parsed = parser(logString);
    var mapped = parsed.map(function(d) {
      return {
        ip: d[0], time: d[2], request: d[3], status: d[4], agent:
          d[8]
      };
    })
    expect(mapped[0].ip).toBe('66.249.64.121');
    expect(mapped[0].time).toBe('22/Nov/2014:01:56:00 +0100');
    expect(mapped[0].request).toBe('GET /robots.txt HTTP/1.1');
    expect(mapped[0].agent).toBe('Mozilla/5.0 (compatible;
      Googlebot/2.1; +http://www.google.com/bot.html)');
    expect(mapped[0].status).toBe('302 507');
  });
});
```

In the preceding code, we use the StringParser service to parse the log string to
an array. After mapping the result to an array of objects, we compare it with the
expected values. The output of Karma should show one successful test, similar to the
following screenshot:

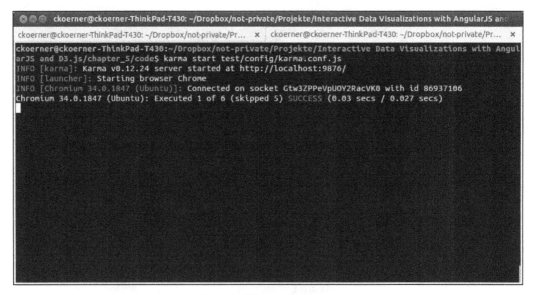

Output of Karma test runner

Grouping log entries

Until now, we parsed all the log entries into an array of readable JavaScript objects. However, when we are visualizing log information, we rather want to display aggregated entries (for example, plotting the amount of people that accessed my application in an interval of 5 minutes) than display all single log entries.

We can achieve this by using the `d3.nest()` function. This function is used to turn a flat data structure into a hierarchical structure based on a single (or multiple) key function. We will use a key function that rounds the time of the log entries to the specified interval (for example, of 5 minutes) and groups all entries of this interval. We are primarily interested in the amount of log entries during this interval, so we can just use the number of entries in the interval. Let's implement this:

```javascript
/* src/app.js */
// Application Module
angular.module('myApp', ['myChart'])
// Main application controller
.controller('MainCtrl', ["$scope", "SimpleHttpLoader",
  "StringParser",
  function ($scope, SimpleHttpLoader, StringParser) {
  var formatter = d3.time.format("%d/%b/%Y:%H:%M:%S %Z");
  $scope.log = {
    src: 'files/access.log',
    data: ''
  };
  SimpleHttpLoader($scope.log.src)
  .then(function(response){
    // Response
    var responseDataStr = response.data;
    // Parse string to an array of datum arrays
    var parsed = StringParser(responseDataStr);
    // Map each datum array to object
    var mapped = parsed.map(function(d) {
      return {
        time: +formatter.parse(d[2]),
        ip: d[0],
        request: d[3],
        status: d[4],
        agent: d[8]
      };
    });
    var grouped = d3.nest()
    .key(function(d){
      // Round to interval of 5 minutes
      var coeff = 1000 * 60 * 5;
      return Math.round(d.time / coeff) * coeff;
```

```
    })
    .entries(mapped);
    $scope.log.data = grouped;
  });
}]);
```

In the preceding code, we added the d3.nest() function to group the data with a specified key function. In our case, the key function rounds the timestamp value (in milliseconds) to an interval of 5 minutes. We can display the result of this grouping with a simple HTML template:

```
<!-- index.html -->
<div ng-controller="MainCtrl">
  <h3>{{ log.src }}</h3>
  <div ng-repeat="l in log.data">
    <span>Key: {{ l.key | date:'medium' }}</span>
    <span>Elements: {{ l.values }}</span>
    <hr>
  </div>
</div>
```

The output of the preceding template can be seen in the following screenshot:

Displaying the grouped log entries

Let's create a small reusable grouping service in the chart module and call it Classifier:

```
/* src/chart.js */
...
```

```
// D3 Classifier service
.factory('Classifier', function(){
  return function(data, key){
    return d3.nest()
      .key(key)
      .entries(data)
      .map(function(d){
        return {
          x: d.key,
          y: d.values.length
        };
      });
  };
}
})
```

In the preceding code, we also added a final mapping function that returns the classifier key as the x property and the number of elements in the group as a y property. This is our internal format for the visualization component.

Testing the classifier

As in the previous services, we want to make sure that the classifier is working properly; therefore, we create a test scenario and a simple test for it. We also want to test the grouping of intervals in a second test. Let's get started:

```
/* test/spec/chart.spec.js */
describe('classifier', function() {
  var elm, scope, classifier, sample;
  beforeEach(module('myChart'));

  beforeEach(inject(function(Classifier) {
    classifier = Classifier;
    sample = [{a:1}, {a:2}, {a:3}];
  }));
  it('should group the data', function() {
    var grouped = classifier(sample, function(d){
      return d.a;
    });
    expect(grouped[0].y).toBe(1);
    expect(grouped[1].y).toBe(1);
    expect(grouped[2].y).toBe(1);
  });
  it('should group the data in an interval', function() {
    var grouped = classifier(sample, function(d){
      var coeff = 2;
      return Math.round(d.a / coeff) * coeff;
```

```
        });
        expect(grouped[0].y).toBe(2);
        expect(grouped[1].y).toBe(1);
    });
});
```

In the preceding code, we injected the `Classifier` service and initialized a sample array of objects. In the following tests, we test the basic grouping operation and the grouping of entries in a certain interval (we define this with the `coeff` variable). The output of the test runner should preferably look similar to the following screenshot:

```
ckoerner@ckoerner-ThinkPad-T430: ~/Dropbox/not-private/Projekte/Interactive Data Visu
ckoerner@ckoerner-ThinkPad-T430:~/Dropbox/not-private/Projekte/Interactive Data V
isualizations with AngularJS and D3.js/chapter_5/code$ karma start test/config/ka
rma.conf.js
INFO [karma]: Karma v0.12.31 server started at http://localhost:9876/
INFO [launcher]: Starting browser Chrome
INFO [Chromium 41.0.2272 (Ubuntu)]: Connected on socket vQ_oWTH8A1X4BFXDUxt9 with
 id 50372043
Chromium 41.0.2272 (Ubuntu): Executed 8 of 8 SUCCESS (0.225 secs / 0.22 secs)
```

Output of Karma test runner

Displaying logs

In the previous sections, we wrote data loading, parsing, and grouping services; now, it's time to use them in a simple example to display the logs. We want to display the number of visitors of our application in an interval of 5 minutes. We define the appearance of the logs directly in the controller as follows:

```
/* src/app.js */
// Application Module
```

```javascript
angular.module('myApp', ['myChart'])
// Main application controller
.controller('MainCtrl', ["$scope", "d3", "SimpleHttpLoader",
  "StringParser", "Classifier", function ($scope, d3,
  SimpleHttpLoader, StringParser, Classifier) {

  // Formats date strings 22/Nov/2014:01:56:00 +0100
  var formatter = d3.time.format("%d/%b/%Y:%H:%M:%S %Z");
  $scope.log = {
    // Source of the log file
    src: 'files/access2.log',

    // Data entries
    data: [],
    // Maps response array to readable JSON object
    map: function(d) {
      return {
        time: +formatter.parse(d[2]),
        ip: d[0],
        request: d[3],
        status: d[4],
        agent: d[8]
      };
    },
    // Group the x-values in an interval of x minutes
    groupByMinutes: 5
  };
  // Load the source file
  SimpleHttpLoader($scope.log.src).then(function(response){
    // Concat all responses to string
    var responseDataStr = response.data;
    // Parse string to an array of datum arrays
    var parsed = StringParser(responseDataStr);

    // Map each datum array to object
    var mapped = parsed.map($scope.log.map);

    // Group the dataset by time
    var grouped = Classifier(mapped, function(d) {
      var coeff = 1000 * 60 * $scope.log.groupByMinutes;
      return Math.round(d.time / coeff) * coeff;
    });
    // Use the grouped data for the chart
    $scope.log.data = grouped;
  });
}]);
```

In the preceding example, we use `SimpleHttpLoader` to load the log file from the server. Then, we parse the log string with the previously implemented `StringParser`. After mapping the array of entries of JavaScript objects, we group them in an interval of 5 minutes using the `Classifier` service and a custom `key` function. Now, let's use the `MyScatterChart` directive from the previous chapter to display the visitors in a chart:

```
<!-- index.html -->
<div ng-controller="MainCtrl">

    <my-scatter-chart class="chart" data="log.data"></my-scatter-
        chart>
</div>
```

The chart should show data points for the number of visitors on the page in an interval of 5 minutes; let's look at the output:

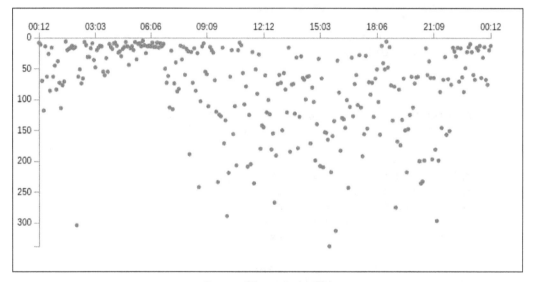

Output of the access log file

Summary

In this chapter, you learned about two different XHR techniques to load external data for the visualization: `d3.xhr` with D3.js and `$http` with AngularJS. If we include an already existing chart application in the AngularJS application, we can wrap the D3.js loading component into a service. In order to test this component, we need to write asynchronous unit tests.

If we write the visualization from scratch, we'd better implement the data loading technique with the $http module of Angular JS. This allows you to mock the behavior of $httpBackend and automatically serve data for specified routes. With this method, we can continue to write synchronous tests, which are more readable and expressive.

In the second part of this chapter, we parsed a string of log entries into an array of JavaScript objects. In addition to the parser service, we implemented a grouping service based on the d3.nest() function. In the end, we brought all the parts together and plotted an aggregated view of the log file with the scatter chart directive of the previous chapter.

In the next chapter, you will learn about drawing paths and shapes with SVG and D3.js. This will help us to extend the current simple scatter chart to a line or area chart.

6
Drawing Curves and Shapes

In the last chapter, you learned how to load, parse, and group real data from the server and we displayed this data in a scatter chart. In this chapter, we will create multiple types of charts to be more flexible in visualizing all the information.

First, we will go through the common shapes in SVG and discuss their usage and attributes. These shapes are easy to use, but solely for simple polygons or ellipses.

In the following section, we will take a look at the more flexible SVG path element and the command to draw lines and curves. After an introduction to Bézier curves, we will be able to draw arbitrary shapes and curves with the SVG commands.

In the third section, we will look at the built-in path generators of D3.js, which facilitate the construction of complex shapes. We will go through a lot of examples to see the different options and parameters in action.

In the last section, we will apply the newly discovered features and implement different chart types for our chart directive. After reading this chapter, it should be very easy to improve the scatter chart of the previous chapters such that it can display lines, areas, bars, or even more complex shapes.

In this chapter you will:

- Learn how to use common SVG shapes
- Learn how to draw polygons with the path element
- Understand the main concepts of Bézier Curves
- Learn how to draw curves and arcs with the path element
- Understand the path generators in D3.js
- Learn how to implement multiple chart types for the chart directive

Common shapes and primitives

Until now, we solely used the `circle` element to draw data points in the chart. However, SVG provides a rich set of more common shapes, which can also be directly used in D3.js. SVG built-in shapes are:

- `rect`
- `circle`
- `ellipse`
- `line`
- `polyline`
- `polygon`

To use built-in shapes in D3.js, we just append them to the SVG node and modify the attributes, just like before with the `circle` element.

> To read more about built-in SVG shapes and their attributes, take a look at the specification at `http://www.w3.org/TR/SVG/shapes.html`.

Let's look at some simple examples. By now, we should have no problems drawing an ellipse. All attributes and their usage can be found in the SVG specification, as shown in the following code:

```
var svg = d3.select("body").append("svg")
  .attr("width", 400)
  .attr("height", 400);

var ellipse = svg.append("ellipse")
  .attr("cx", 200)
  .attr("cy", 200)
  .attr("rx", 180)
  .attr("ry", 90);
```

The output of the code in the browser looks like the following screenshot:

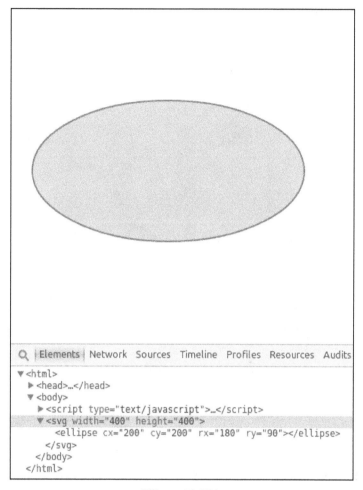

Ellipse with D3.js

In the preceding screenshot, we see that D3.js does exactly what we expected it to do; it creates the `ellipse` node and assigns the `cx`, `cy`, `rx`, and `ry` attributes. You learned already in the previous chapters that we can use all attributes of the underlying SVG standard with D3.js. Therefore, we can also easily draw a rectangle with round corners by just using the proper attributes of `rect` as follows:

```
var svg = d3.select("body").append("svg")
    .attr("width", 400)
    .attr("height", 400);

var rect = svg.append("rect")
```

```
.attr("x", 10)
.attr("y", 110)
.attr("width", 380)
.attr("height", 180)
.attr("rx", 50);
```

Rectangle with round corners in D3.js

In the preceding screenshot, we can see that the rx attribute is responsible for the corner radius. However, what if we want to be more flexible and want to draw an arbitrary polygon. The SVG polygon element uses a points attribute that stores a list of all the points that are connected by the polygon. The format of the points is: x1, y1 x2, y2 x3, y3, and so on, whereas for the polygon primitive, the last point is automatically connected to the starting point. Let's look at an example:

```
var svg = d3.select("body").append("svg")
  .attr("width", 800)
  .attr("height", 400);

var polygon = svg.append("polygon")
  .attr("points", "350,75  379,161 469,161 397,215 423,301 350,250
277,301 303,215 231,161 321,161");
```

In the preceding example, we see that in order to draw a star-shaped polygon, we need to connect 10 points and the starting point with straight lines.

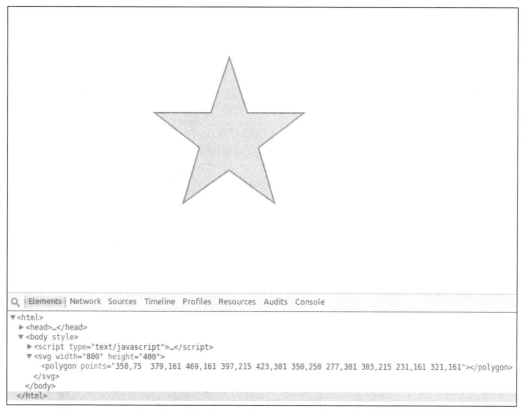

Star-shaped polygon and its corresponding DOM tree

In the preceding screenshot, we see that the star-shaped polygon is the result of connecting 10 points from the points attribute and the starting point by straight lines.

Curved lines with the SVG path

What if we need to draw with curved lines? Now, we will be able to draw all possible polygons, but we lack the possibility of drawing more complex shapes (such as curves and polynomial functions). Fortunately, the SVG standard provides a very flexible element for this called the path element. With this element, one can draw the most flexible curves and shapes as well as all the previous common shapes.

The path element takes a d attribute to define the exact shape of the path. The shape can be defined with special commands (such as drawing straight line, drawing smooth curve, and so on) and point coordinates.

Let us first look at the preceding example; we want to draw the same star-shaped polygon, but this time with the use of the `path` element, as shown in the following code:

```
var svg = d3.select("body").append("svg")
  .attr("width", 800)
  .attr("height", 400);

var polygon = svg.append("path")
  .attr("d", 'M350,75  L379,161 469,161 397,215 423,301 350,250
277,301 303,215 231,161 321,161 z');
```

In the preceding code, we wrote the exact same 10 points as before to the d attribute of the `path` element and added some additional characters M, L, and z. These characters are actual commands that are used to interpret the subsequent coordinates, as we'll see in the following screenshot:

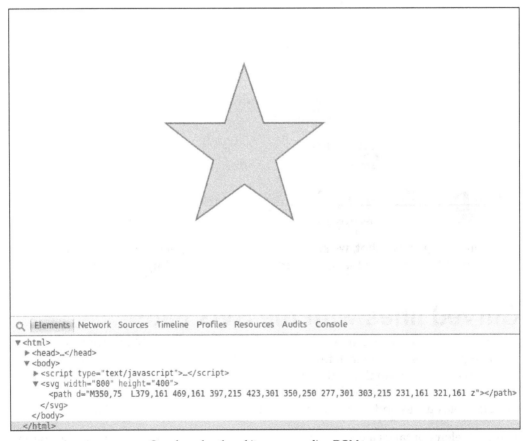

Star-shaped path and its corresponding DOM tree

In the preceding screenshot, we see that the shape looks exactly the same, but is now defined via a `path` element and a `d` attribute. So, what shapes can be drawn in SVG and which commands need to be used?

In the SVG standard, the following commands are available to draw. Don't worry if this looks complicated; I will give examples for these commands right after the following list:

- `M` (*moveto*): This sets the starting point for a new curve: `M x0, y0`.

- `L` (*lineto*): This connects the previous and the first coordinates with a straight line: `...x0, y0 L x1, y1`.

- `H` (*horizontal lineto*): This connects the previous and the first x coordinate with a horizontal line: `...x0, y0 H x1`.

- `V` (*vertical lineto*): This connects the previous and the first y coordinate with a vertical line: `...x0, y0 V y1`.

- `C` (*curveto*): This connects the previous point and the third coordinates with a cubic Bézier curve using the first two as control points: `...x0, y0 C x1, y1 x2, y2 x3, y3`.

- `S` (*smooth curveto*): This connects the previous point and the second coordinates with a cubic Bézier curve. It reflects the last control point and uses the first point as a new control point: `...x0, y0 S x1, y1 x2, y2`.

- `Q` (*quadratic curveto*): This connects the previous point and the second coordinates with a quadratic Bézier curve. It uses the first point as control point: `...x0, y0 Q x1, y1 x2, y2`.

- `T` (*smooth quadratic curveto*): This connects the previous point and the first coordinates with a quadratic Bézier curve. It reflects the last control point: `...x0, y0 T x1, y1`.

- `A` (*elliptical arc*): This connects the previous and the fourth coordinates with an ellipse using the first coordinates as radius in the x and y direction, the second value as rotation around the x axis, and the third coordinates as large arc and sweep flags: `...x0, y0 A x1, y1 x2 x3, y3 x4, y4`.

- `Z` (*closepath*): This connects the previous point and the starting point with a straight line: `...x0, y0 Z`.

All paths have to start with the `M` moveto command and in all these commands, capital letters assume the coordinates are absolute and small letters assume the coordinates are relative to the previous point.

Drawing straight lines

Drawing straight lines with the SVG commands is very simple. We define starting coordinates with the M moveto command and then continue adding coordinates to the L lineto command. This will simply connect the points with lines. Let's look at an example:

```
var line1 = svg.append("path")
    .style("stroke", 'steelblue')
    .attr("d", 'M10,10  L100,100 300,100 400,10');
```

In the following figure, we can see the resulting graphic. To better see the points that define the shape, I added little circles to the coordinates:

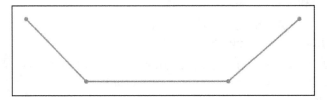

Line path with lineto

In order to not fill the area, I added a small styling to the examples:

```
<style type="text/css">
path {
   stroke-width: 2;
   fill: none;
}
circle {
   stroke: none
}
</style>
```

Let's add two horizontal lines at the top and bottom of the previous shape; we just need to define one x coordinate, as shown in the following code:

```
var hline1 = svg.append("path")
  .style("stroke", 'red')
  .attr("d", 'M10,1  H400');
var hline2 = svg.append("path")
  .style("stroke", 'red')
  .attr("d", 'M10,110  H400');
```

Line path with horizontal lineto

Let's add two vertical lines on the left-hand side and the right-hand side of the previous shape; we solely need to define one y coordinate as follows:

```
var vline1 = svg.append("path")
  .style("stroke", 'green')
  .attr("d", 'M1,0 V110');
var vline2 = svg.append("path")
  .style("stroke", 'green')
  .attr("d", 'M410,0  V110');
```

Line path with vertical lineto

Bézier curves

Modeling polynomial functions and curves with cubic or quadratic polynomials in the shape of the following expression is neither easy nor intuitive:

$$f(x) = a \cdot x^3 + b \cdot x^2 + c \cdot x + d$$

Modifying the coefficients in such a function to draw and design a shape is nearly impossible because the change of a coefficient results in a very unpredictable change of the function value. However, fortunately, Bézier and De Casteljau developed the concept of Bézier curves in the 60s. Bézier curves use easy-to-model control points and binomial expansion to derive a parametric function as a sum of polynomials with the following formula:

$$f(t) = \sum_{i=0}^{n} B_{i,n}(t) \cdot P_i$$

B is the so-called Bernstein polynomial and it has the following shape:

$$B_{i,n}(t) = \binom{n}{i} t^i (1-t)^{n-i}$$

P^i is the control points to model the curve. Let's write the cubic polynomial function from the preceding code in this shape; we get the following parametric function:

$$f(t) = (1-t)^3 \cdot P_0 + 3t(1-t)^2 \cdot P_1 + 3t^2(1-t) \cdot P_2 + t^3 \cdot P_3$$

This resulting polynomial describes a cubic function that is interpolated between the four control points: P_0, P_1, P_2, and P_3. The t parameter in the range 0 to 1 defines the position on the curve between the starting point P_0 (in the figure **P1**) and the end point P_3 (in the figure **P2**); P_1 (in the figure **C1**) and P_2 (in the figure **C2**) are called control points and are used to model the shape between these points. Let's visualize this:

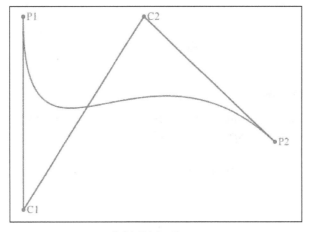

Cubic Bézier Curve

We can immediately see the advantage of this representation: The control points P^i can be directly used to model the cubic function. Changes in the control points result in predictable changes in the function values.

The interpolation of the function can be easily implemented with the recursive De Casteljau algorithm, which I am doing graphically for t = 0.1, 0.25, 0.5, 0.75, and 0.9 in the following figure. We connect P_0, P_1, P_2, and P_3 with straight lines and find the relative position t on these lines. This gives three new points, which we again connect with straight lines and do the same as before until we are left with a single point (after three iterations). This point is the desired point on the curve for a given parameter t.

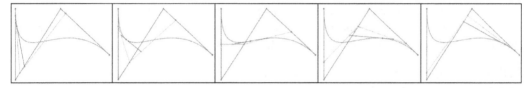

De Casteljau algorithm for cubic polynomial evaluated at t = 0.1, 0.25, 0.5, 0.75, and 0.9

For quadratic polynomials (order 2), we have solely one control point. Let's also visualize this example:

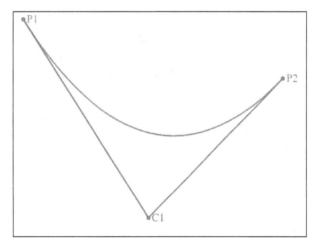

Quadratic Bézier Curve

We can again use the De Casteljau algorithm to interpolate the quadratic function graphically for t = 0.1, 0.25, 0.5, 0.75, and 0.9:

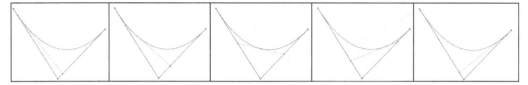

De Casteljau algorithm for quadratic polynomial evaluated at t = 0.1, 0.25, 0.5, 0.75, and 0.9

When doing this for the first time, the transition from polynomial functions to parametric Bézier curves seems a bit complicated; this is absolutely normal. The important message here is that we are interpolating the curve between start points, end points, and control points. This lets us easily modify the shape of these curves by moving the control points in the desired directions.

Let's look at the actual implementation of the cubic and quadratic curves from the preceding example with D3.js and SVG:

```
var cubic = svg.append("path")
  .attr("d", 'M15,15  C15,300 200,15 400,200');
var quadratic = svg.append("path")
  .attr("d", 'M15,15  Q200,300 400,100');
```

In the preceding code, we see that the cubic Bézier curve takes the starting *moveto* command, then 2 control points, and one end point with the *curveto* command. In comparison, the quadratic curve takes one control point and one end point with the *quadratic curveto* command.

Both the commands: *smooth curveto* and *quadratic smooth curveto* allows smooth connections of multiple Bézier curve segments by reflecting the previous control point in the new segment. The connection is only perfectly smooth if the reflected control point of the previous end point is used as a control point for the new starting point.

Let's look at some example, where we construct two quadratic Bézier curves, one without *smooth curveto* and a control point and the other with *smooth curveto* and without a control point:

```
var quadratic1 = svg.append("path")
  .attr("d", 'M15,15  Q200,300 400,100 Q500,50 800,100');
var quadratic2 = svg.append("path")
  .attr("d", 'M15,215  Q200,500 400,300 T800,300');
```

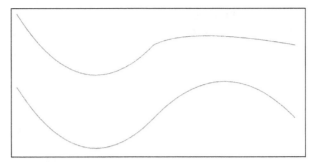

Two quadratic Bézier curves: normal segments (top), smooth segments (bottom)

In the preceding figure, we see that solely with reflected control points, the transition between the two segments of quadratic Bézier curves is smooth.

Drawing ellipses and elliptical arcs

The *elliptical arc* command can be used to draw segments of ellipses. The configuration allows you to define the starting point of the segment, radius in x and y direction, rotation around the x axis, large arc and sweep flag, and ending point of the segment.

The only new options here are the two flags. The large arc flags define if the arc is connected via the shorter or the larger side and the sweep flag mirrors the shape. Let's look at all possible variations:

```
var arc1 = svg.append("path")
  .style("stroke", 'red')
  .attr("d", 'M50,200  A150,100 0 0,0 300,100');

var arc2 = svg.append("path")
  .style("stroke", 'green')
  .attr("d", 'M50,200  A150,100 0 1,0 300,100');

var arc3 = svg.append("path")
  .style("stroke", 'orange')
  .attr("d", 'M50,200  A150,100 0 0,1 300,100');

var arc4 = svg.append("path")
  .style("stroke", 'blue')
  .attr("d", 'M50,200  A150,100 0 1,1 300,100');
```

In the following figure, we see the output of the preceding code. Red and orange are small arcs — where orange is mirrored — and blue and green are large arcs — where blue is mirrored:

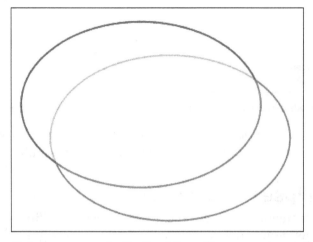

The elliptical arc command with all variations of large arc and sweep flags

Path generators in D3.js

Designing and defining custom paths with plain SVG commands is possible, but difficult and very uncomfortable. Fortunately, D3.js provides very useful methods to generate the d attribute of the `path` element for different shapes. Once we know what the magic is behind these generators, we can use them to abstract all the SVG commands and to work directly on the datasets.

Generating straight lines

We can create a line generator by calling the `d3.svg.line()` function. This will return a function, which generates the SVG command for the path of the shape. Let's try a simple example:

```
var points =[[15,15], [200, 300], [400,100]];

var line = d3.svg.line();

var path1 = svg.append("path")
  .datum(points)
  .attr("d", line);
```

In the preceding code, we observe that we solely plug the line generator returned by `d3.svg.line()` in the d attribute. As a result, the line generator will be invoked for every point that is defined in the `.datum()` function. The output of the code looks like the following figure:

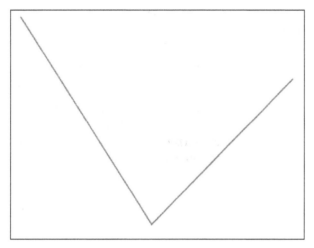

Output of the line generated with the line generator

The big advantage here is that we can continue to work with our data arrays without caring about the actual SVG command. To transform the straight line into a smooth curve, we need to solely add an interpolation option to the line generator as follows:

```
var points =[[15,15], [200, 300], [400,100]];

var line = d3.svg.line();

var path1 = svg.append("path")
  .datum(points)
  .style("stroke", 'green')
  .attr("d", line.interpolate('cardinal').tension(0));

var path2 = svg.append("path")
  .datum(points)
  .style("stroke", 'yellow')
  .attr("d", line.interpolate('cardinal').tension(0.25));

var path3 = svg.append("path")
  .datum(points)
  .style("stroke", 'orange')
  .attr("d", line.interpolate('cardinal').tension(0.5));
```

```
var path4 = svg.append("path")
  .datum(points)
  .style("stroke", 'red')
  .attr("d", line.interpolate('cardinal').tension(0.75));

var path4 = svg.append("path")
  .datum(points)
  .style("stroke", 'steelblue')
  .attr("d", line.interpolate('cardinal').tension(1));
```

In the preceding code, we observe an `.interpolate()` function and a `.tension()` function. The `.interpolate()` function defines the current interpolation method for the current shape and the `.tension()` function sets the tension of the interpolated curve. We use the smooth cardinal interpolation that works very similar to the Bézier curves concept of interpolation between control points. Let's look at the resulting image:

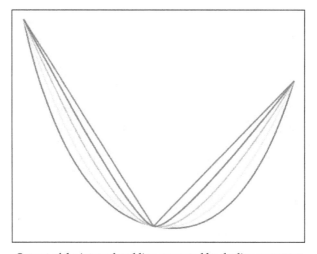

Output of the interpolated line generated by the line generator

There are various predefined interpolation functions (such as linear, step, monotone, and so on). These can be found in the D3.js documentation.

Generate paths for areas

Similar to the line generator, we can also create the SVG commands for an area; to do so, we can use the `d3.svg.area()` function. Let's create an example area:

```
var points =[[15,15], [200, 300], [400,100]];

var area = d3.svg.area()
  .y0(390);
```

```
var shape1 = svg.append("path")
    .datum(points)
    .attr("d", area);
```

In the previous code, we see that we can call an additional `.y0()` method to the generator that defines the y boundaries of the area. Let's look at the outputted figure:

Output of the area generated with the area generator

We can also use dynamic properties in the `.y0()` method and the same interpolation functions as in the previous section. Let's apply both of these in the next example:

```
var points =[[15,15], [200, 300], [400,100]];

var area = d3.svg.area()
    .y0(function(d){ return d[1]+90; });

var shape1 = svg.append("path")
    .datum(points)
    .attr("d", area.interpolate('cardinal'));
```

In the preceding code, we see that using the `.datum()` method allows you to also use dynamic properties in the generator function.

As expected, the connections between the points are interpolated now and also the second boundary changes with every data point. We can see the expected results in the following figure:

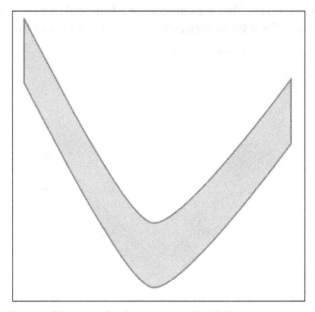

Output of the interpolated area generated with the area generator

Generating arcs

Until now, we solely used Cartesian coordinates to define lines and curves. Another huge feature of D3.js is that it includes a lot of projection and conversion tools (such as the arc generator). The `d3.svg.arc()` arc generator can be designed with the starting and ending angle as well as the inner and outer radius. Let's look at an easy example:

```
var arc = d3.svg.arc()
    .innerRadius(40)
    .outerRadius(100)
    .startAngle(0)
    .endAngle(1);

var shape1 = svg.append("path")
    .attr("d", arc)
    .attr("transform", 'translate(200,200)');
```

The resulting graphic shows an arc as we defined it in the preceding code. We see that angles are measured in radiant, and we need to move the center of the arc to the visible area. The resulting figure looks like this:

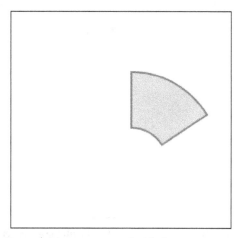

Output of the arc generated with the arc generator

We can also draw multiple arc segments and use dynamic properties on the arc, for example, to change the angle. Let's try this:

```
var points =[[0,15,'red'], [20, 90,'green'], [110,180,'orange']];

var arc = d3.svg.arc()
  .innerRadius(40)
  .outerRadius(100)
  .startAngle(function(d){return d[0] * Math.PI/180;})
  .endAngle(function(d){return d[1] * Math.PI/180;});

var shape1 = svg.selectAll("path")
  .data(points)
  .enter().append("path")
  .attr("d", arc)
  .style("fill", function(d) { return d[2]; })
  .attr("transform", 'translate(200,200)');
```

We add the dataset via the `.data()` method and generate arcs for every element in the dataset. Then, we define the starting and ending angles depending on the elements in the dataset. The resulting figure looks like the following figure:

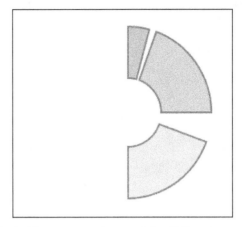

Output of the arc segments generated with the arc generator

Different chart types

Now, we are finally ready to improve the scatter chart directive from the previous chapters. In this section, we will define a base chart that displays points, lines, the area of the graph, and bar charts, which displays a bar for each value.

Implementing line charts

Let's refresh how we previously drew the data points on the screen. We added the dataset in the `.data()` function because we wanted to draw one point per data value. We also need to scale the x and y coordinates of the data points according to our previously defined linear scaling:

```
/* src/chart.js */
svg.select('.data')
  .selectAll('circle').data(data)
  .enter()
  .append('circle')
  .attr('class', 'data-point');

svg.select('.data')
  .selectAll('circle').data(data)
  .attr('r', 2.5)
  .attr('cx', function(d) { return xScale(d.x); })
  .attr('cy', function(d) { return yScale(d.y); });
```

This was pretty easy. Now, we want to draw a smooth line that connects all data points and interpolates the space in between. First, we need to define a line generator. This generator returns the proper x and y coordinates. Then, we add the `cardinal` interpolation.

Finally, we can add the dataset in the `.datum()` method because we want to draw solely one line (but with multiple points):

```
/* src/chart.js */
var line = d3.svg.line()
    .x(function(d) { return xScale(d.x); })
    .y(function(d) { return yScale(d.y); })
    .interpolate('cardinal');

svg.select(".data-line")
    .datum(data)
    .attr("d", line);
```

As a last step, we want to fill the area under the graph. Similar to the previous line generator, we define an area generator and all its accessors. Then, we add the dataset along with the `.datum()` function to the path element and autogenerate an area path element:

```
/* src/chart.js */
var area = d3.svg.area()
    .x(function(d) { return xScale(d.x); })
    .y0(yScale(0))
    .y1(function(d) { return yScale(d.y); })
    .interpolate('cardinal');

svg.select(".data-area")
    .datum(data)
    .attr("d", area);
```

In the following figure of a real Apache access log, we can see the result of the newly created base chart:

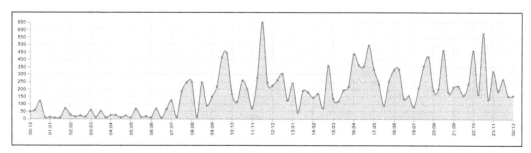

Base chart (points, line, and area)

Drawing lines and areas is a matter of three lines of code, but it's important to understand what's going on under the hood. When creating custom interpolation or customized adjustments, we may have to dig in the path element and get our hands dirty. Then, it's absolutely necessary to know the basics of SVG paths and Bézier curves.

Designing bar charts

Creating bar charts is also very straightforward. We need to draw a rectangle for every data point with a certain width and height. The best way is to start first with computing the width of a single bar by dividing the available width by a number of required bars (a number of data points).

Now, we can define the x coordinate and the width without problems. The y coordinate and the height are a little bit tricky, as we are drawing from the top to the bottom. So, we need to switch these values and draw to the difference of the maximum value minus the current coordinate:

```
/* src/chart.js */
var barWidth = (width-2*margin)/data.length;

svg.select('.data')
  .selectAll('rect').data(data)
  .enter()
  .append('rect')
  .attr('class', 'data-bar');

svg.select('.data')
  .selectAll('rect').data(data)
  .attr('r', 2.5)
  .attr('x', function(d) { return xScale(d.x) - barWidth*0.5; })
  .attr('y', function(d) { return yScale(d.y); })
  .attr('width', function(d) { return barWidth; })
  .attr('height', function(d) { return yScale(0) - yScale(d.y);
});
```

Once implemented, the resulting bar chart looks like this:

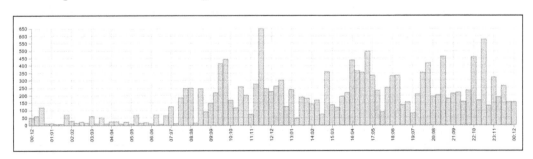

Bar chart

Summary

In this chapter, you learned the basics of SVG curves and shapes and how they are generated in D3.js.

In the first section, we saw common shapes such as rectangles (with round corners), ellipses, polygons, and so on. These shapes are very easy to construct because they take a small number of self explaining arguments. The polygon element is the most flexible common shape because we can connect an arbitrary number of data points with straight lines to a shape. Next, we saw the various commands responsible for drawing curves and lines with the path element. Every line starts with the *moveto* command and takes an arbitrary number of commands and coordinates. We saw the *lineto* and *curveto* commands as well as *elliptic arcs*.

This chapter also contained a small introduction to the origin of Bézier curves as a parametric version for polynomial functions with the use of binomial expansion. This enables us to modify the shape of the polynomial function with start, end, and control points rather than the plain coefficients.

Later, we discussed the built-in path generator functions of D3.js. These can be used to easily generate complex, flexible curves, and shapes.

In the last section, we extended the base chart directive so that it can also display points, lines, and areas. Theoretically, we could implement various arbitrary shapes for our chart directives. As a second example, we implemented bar charts directive by just placing rectangle elements on the proper positions of the chart.

In the next chapter, we will take a closer look at transitions, animations, and implement update transitions for all our directives. Animating chart updates will make it not only easier to see when an update occurred, but will also make it more fancy and intuitive. We can make much more sense of data, for example, if new data slides in from the right-hand side and old data slides out to the left.

7
Controlling Transitions and Animations

In the previous chapters, you learned how to generate different charts from server log data such as scatter charts, line charts, area charts, and so on. If we want to update the chart to display the most recent logs, we will simply have to redraw the whole chart. However, this will make it very difficult to see where and how the changes affected the visualization. In this chapter, we will take a close look at transitions and animations as a way to visualize and better understand the data changes.

First, we will start with an introduction to animations in D3.js that consist of timers and interpolations. This will give us a good notion to understand how D3.js processes animations under the hood.

In the second section, you will learn more about transitions, a special kind of animation that solely describe the change from one state to another. With previous knowledge, we will understand how timers and interpolations internally work for transitions. We will also see examples for staggered and chained transitions and how to design plausible transitions.

Whenever attributes cannot be automatically interpolated, we need to use custom interpolation functions; to use them in the transitions we need tweens, a form of customized transitions. In this section, you will learn how to design a simple attribute tween function to animate the area of a path element.

After learning about linear transitions, you will learn about easing and easing functions in computer graphics. With the introduction of Bezier curves in the previous chapter, it will be straightforward to understand and design custom easing functions with D3.js.

At the end of this chapter, we will apply the acquired skills to implement different transitions for the previously designed charts.

In this chapter, you will:

- Learn about animations with timers and interpolations
- Create staggered and chained transitions
- Understand when to use animations
- Implement simple attribute tweens
- Understand easing functions
- Implement transitions for multiple chart types

Animations

In data visualizations, animations are a way to visualize changes in the dataset, which makes it much easier to see, understand, and follow the data changes. An animation usually consists of timed key frames that represent these changes over time in the visualization. Now, we will go through an animation step by step and see the different things that need to be considered when creating a custom animation.

Let's look at a simple example. In the following figure, we can see an animation built by six key frames to create an illusion of a color transition from blue to red:

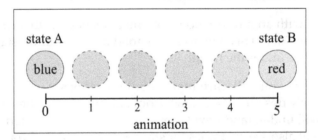

Animation with 6 key frames

Timer in D3.js with d3.timer

To implement this animation, D3.js provides an efficient and smart timer queue. This lets you run multiple concurrent timers. To create a timer, we can simply call the d3.timer(tickFn[, delay[, time]]) function. The delay and time arguments let you schedule the start of the timer after a certain delay of milliseconds or at a specific point in time.

The first argument: `tickFn` is the callback function that is executed every time the timer is updated. The `tickFn(elapsed)` callback function is internally called with the elapsed time in milliseconds as argument. The timer only stops if the callback returns `true` and cannot be canceled in any other way.

 D3.js uses the native `requestAnimationFrame()` method if available, which times your animation smoothly with about 60 FPS.

Let's implement the example from the preceding figure and implement a circle and a tick function that changes the color of the circle after every 100 milliseconds from blue to red in five frames:

```
var svg = d3.select("body").append("svg")
    .attr("width", 800)
    .attr("height", 400);

var circle = svg.append("circle")
    .attr("class", "frame")
    .attr("cx", 50)
    .attr("cy", 50)
    .attr("r", 25);

var tickFn = function(elapsed){

    // Frame 0
    if (elapsed <= 100) {
        circle.style("fill", "rgb(0,0,255)");
    }

    // Frame 1
    else if (elapsed <= 200) {
        circle.style("fill", "rgb(50,0,200)");
    }

    // Frame 2
    else if (elapsed <= 300) {
        circle.style("fill", "rgb(75,0,150)");
    }

    // Frame 3
    else if (elapsed <= 400) {
        circle.style("fill", "rgb(150,0,75)");
    }

    // Frame 4
```

```
      else if (elapsed <= 500) {
        circle.style("fill", "rgb(200,0,50)");
      }

      // Frame 5
      else {
        circle.style("fill", "rgb(255,0,0)");

        /* End Timer */
        return true;
      }
    }
```

To start the timer, we need to simply add the following line:

```
    // Start timer
    d3.timer(tickFn);
```

When we run this example, we see the exact same change of the color from blue to red as in the previous figure. The first thing that we realize when looking at the code is that we manually interpolated the color values between blue and red. In the next step, we will look at parametric interpolation.

Interpolation with D3.js

Manually interpolating the colors is not really a good idea; D3.js provides a broad set of functions to interpolate different variables: numbers, strings, colors as well as arrays and objects.

Interpolators are generated by calling the corresponding interpolator constructor, for example, d3.interpolateRgb(a, b) (where a and b are both d3.rgb objects). This interpolator constructor returns an interpolation function interpolate(t) with the parametric argument t. For t equals 0, the result of the interpolation is a, for t equals 1, the result of the interpolation is b, and between 0 and 1, a and b are interpolated. Let's see the example for our previous animation:

```
    var blue = d3.rgb(0,0,255);
    var red = d3.rgb(255,0,0);
    var interpolate = d3.interpolateRgb(blue, red);
```

We can now rewrite the tick function to set the interpolated color values in the frames as follows:

```
    var tickFn = function(elapsed){

      // Frame 0
```

```
    if (elapsed <= 100) {
      circle.style("fill", interpolate(0));
    }

    // Frame 1
    else if (elapsed <= 200) {
      circle.style("fill", interpolate(1/5));
    }

    // Frame 2
    else if (elapsed <= 300) {
      circle.style("fill", interpolate(2/5));
    }

    // Frame 3
    else if (elapsed <= 400) {
      circle.style("fill", interpolate(3/5));
    }

    // Frame 4
    else if (elapsed <= 500) {
      circle.style("fill", interpolate(4/5));
    }

    // Frame 5
    else {
      circle.style("fill", interpolate(1));

      /* End Timer */
      return true;
    }
  }
```

In the next step, we will use all the frames that the tick function provides, not only the five key frames as before. This can be done by simply defining the t interpolation parameter as the ratio of elapsed time and animation duration:

```
var duration = 500;

var tickFn = function(elapsed) {

  var t = elapsed/duration;

  if (t <= 1.0) {
    circle.style("fill", interpolate(t));
```

```
    }
    else {
      circle.style("fill", interpolate(1));

      /* End Timer */
      return true;
    }
  }
}
```

When we compare the preceding code with the previous examples, we can see that it's much more elegant and the animation looks much smoother because we are using the available frame rate of the tick function for the color change animation.

In this example, we have seen a very simple animation, the change from one color to another and the transition from one state to another state. In D3.js, there is a much easier and cleaner way to describe transitions than using timers and interpolations; we will discuss this in the following section.

Easy animations with transitions

Transitions are a special kind of animations where solely the change (transition) between two discrete values—so called states—is described. We can simply think of the previous animation example, a 1-dimensional dataset with the values blue and red, where these two values are interpolated during the animation period. In this previous example of the first section, we started from a custom animation and ended up step by step with a transition between these two states:

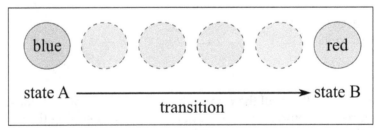

Transition between two states

In D3.js, we call the .transition() method on a Selection to create a transition object, which is again very similar to a Selection itself. This means that we can apply methods like .attr(), .style(), .delay(), and .duration() on this transition object to create automatically interpolated state transitions. Let's take a look at this in action and see how the previous example looks with the usage of transitions:

```
var blue =  d3.rgb(0,0,255);
var red = d3.rgb(255,0,0);
```

```
var duration = 500;

circle
   .style("fill", blue)
   .transition()
   .duration(duration)
   .style("fill", red);
```

In the preceding code, we can see that .duration() and .style() are called on the transition object, which is returned by the .transition() method. This is a much cleaner way to describe the animation of a change from one state to another state. We keep in mind that all the values that we set on the transition object are automatically interpolated by D3.js within the duration period.

D3.js uses the appropriate interpolator to interpolate the property values, interpolateRgb for color values, interpolateNumber for number values, or interpolateString that interpolates numbers embedded in strings.

Staggered transitions

Most of the time when animating multiple elements, we don't want to animate all elements at the same time. It's much easier to follow the animation if it's staggered in time.

We can also use dynamic properties for transition methods such as the .delay() or .duration() method. Let's create staggered transitions for multiple elements where each transition is delayed. We can see this example in the following figure:

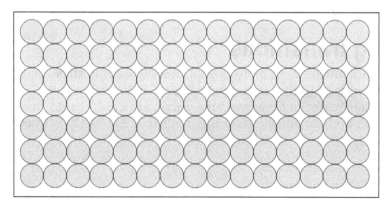

Delayed transitions

In the code of the delayed transitions, we need to add dynamic properties in the `.delay()` function:

```
var blue =  d3.rgb(0,0,255);
var red = d3.rgb(255,0,0);
var duration = 2500;
// elements per row
var epr = 15;

var data = [];
for (var i=0; i<105; i++) {
  data.push(i);
}

var circles = svg.selectAll("circle")
    .data(data).enter()
    .append("circle")
    .attr("class", "frame")
    .attr("cx", function(d,i) { return (i%epr + 1)*50; })
    .attr("cy", function(d,i) { return Math.floor(i/epr + 1)*50; })
    .attr("r", 25);

circles
    .style("fill", blue)
    .transition()
    .delay(function(d,i) { return i*100; })
    .duration(duration)
    .style("fill", red);
```

Chaining transitions

In most cases, it's much easier, more elegant, and more comfortable to create an animation by piecing together transitions rather than to deal with timers and interpolations manually. In D3.js, we can use the `.each(callback)` method on the transition object to chain transitions or the `.each(event, callback)` event handler to listen for `start`, `end`, or `interrupt` events.

If we want to detect the end of a transition, we need to add the `.each(event, callback)` event listener to the selection of circles and listen for the `end` event of each transition of the circles. Whenever the event occurs, the callback function is executed. In the scope of the callback function, the `this` variable holds the reference to the current element of the Selection whose event was triggered. The element can be easily transformed to a D3-Selection by calling `d3.select(this)`. Let's extend the previous example, as shown in the following code:

```
circles
  .style("fill", blue)
  .transition()
  .delay(function(d,i) { return i*100; })
  .duration(duration)
  .style("fill", red)
  .each("end", function(){
    d3.select(this)
      .transition()
      .attr("r", 15);
  });
```

In the preceding code, we wait for each element to finish the color transition, and in a subsequent step, we start a new transition that shrinks the radius of the current element down to `15px`. We can see the resulting animation of the preceding code in the following figure:

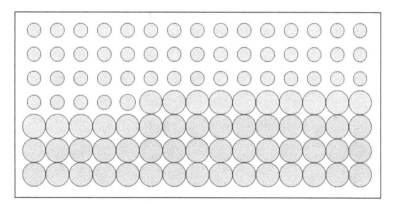

Event handler detects end of transition

Creating plausible transitions

As we discussed before, animations should help the reader to make sense of data changes; thus, animations and transitions should be solely used to visualize the data changes in a plausible way.

In general, we distinguish three common transitions for state changes in data visualizations (see the following figure):

- **Enter transitions**: Here, data is added to the visualization
- **Update transitions**: Here, data is updated in the visualization
- **Exit transitions**: Here, data is removed from the visualization

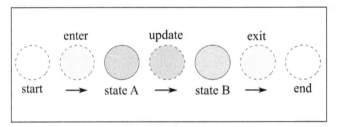

Data value transition

In contrast to data value transitions, we can also animate the transition between two different data representation styles, for example, the transition from a bar chart to a pie chart. These transitions change the representation type of the data where the data remains the same. In the following figure, we can see an example where the data representation is changed from a circle to a rectangle:

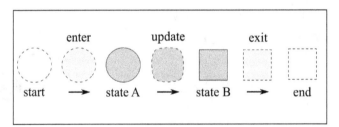

Data representation transition

Both methods — value transitions and representation transitions — should never be mixed together in one single transition.

Interpolate anything with tweens

When dealing with complex properties in transitions, for example, line and area functions that generate the d attribute, automatic interpolations can get a bit tricky. This can especially cause problems when D3.js does not have any proper interpolation for the desired properties. In these cases, we need to use a custom interpolation function for the attribute transition; this is called tween in D3.js. We can either use attrTween(attr, tweenFn), styleTween(style, tweenFn), or a tween factory tween(name, factory) to create custom interpolators. Let's switch back to the AngularJS project where you already learned to display area charts. In order to create animations for the area chart, we need to interpolate the points of the dataset. Let's first draw the area with the following code:

```
var area = d3.svg.area()
   .x(function(d) { return xScale(d.x); })
   .y0(yScale(0))
   .y1(function(d) { return yScale(d.y); })
   .interpolate('cardinal');
svg.select(".data-area")
   .datum(data)
   .attr("d", area);
```

The preceding code will create an output similar to the following screenshot:

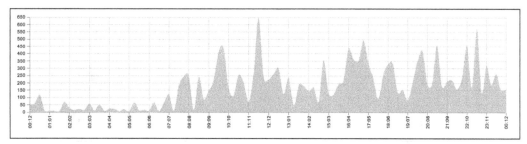

Area chart generated with area function

To animate the d attribute, we need a custom interpolation function that can interpolate the array of objects that is passed to the area generator; thus, we need to use tweens. Let's implement an interpolation function interpolatePoints for arrays of objects in the form of {x:0,y:0};:

```
var interpolatePoints = function(A, B) {

   var interpolator_x = d3.interpolateArray(
      A.map(function(d){ return d.x; }),
      B.map(function(d){ return d.x; })
   );
```

```
    var interpolator_y = d3.interpolateArray(
      A.map(function(d){ return d.y; }),
      B.map(function(d){ return d.y; })
    );

    return function(t) {
      var x = interpolator_x(t);
      var y = interpolator_y(t);

      return x.map(function(d,i){
        return {
          x: x(i),
          y: y(i)
        };
      });
    };
  };
```

The preceding code combines the x and y values to arrays and runs the array interpolation function on them. Then, it returns an interpolation function, which combines both the interpolated arrays, back to an array of objects.

Let's assume we want to create a transition that grows the area in the direction of the *y* axis, similar to the following screenshot:

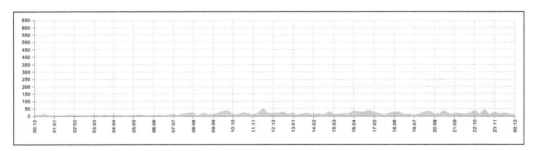

Attribute tween transition in an area chart

We can achieve this by creating an attrTween function for the d attribute and returning an interpolated value between an array with all y values, 0, and the data array. The code will look like this:

```
svg.select(".data-area")
  .datum(data)
  .transition()
  .duration(duration)
  .attrTween("d", function(){

    var min = d3.min(data, function(d){ return d.y; });
```

```
var start = data.map(function(d){
  return {
    x: d.x,
    y: min
  };
});

var interpolate = interpolatePoints(start, data);

return function(t) {
  return area(interpolate(t));
};
});
```

In the preceding code, we grow the area in the direction of the y axis. First in the `attrTween` function, we create a `start` array. This stores the correct x values and the minimum y value of the dataset. Then, we create the custom interpolation function between the `start` array and the dataset. In the end, we return the interpolated `area` function.

Realistic animations with easing

Until now, we animated all attribute changes with the same time step size. However, all physical realistic animations are accelerated or decelerated; therefore, the animation over time is not linear anymore. If we want to create plausible and realistic animations, we have to adapt the linear step size with a nonlinear easing function.

Easing functions describe the change of a value over time, where value is the property that we want to animate. Let's imagine the transition of a ball from position 0 (left-hand side) to position 1 (right-hand side), the ball moves from left to right. If the ball moves with a constant speed from left to right, we call it a linear transition (or linear easing).

We can also visualize this. Let's assume that the whole animation takes 1 second and every 0.2 seconds we take a picture of the ball in the scene. We can see that the position changes linearly with a step size of 0.2 because of the constant speed. We can see this linear transition in the following figure:

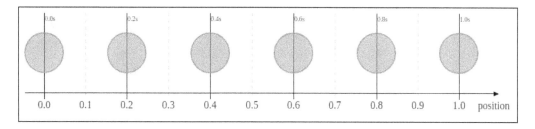

Let's look at this transition in a 2D chart where we plot the time on the x-axis and the position of the ball on the y-axis (see the following figure). This plot is the so-called easing function, in this case, the linear easing function that describes the change of the animation value (here, the position) over time:

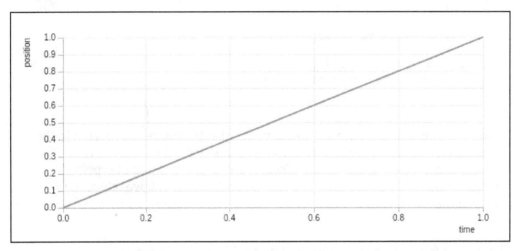

Linear easing function

Let's assume that the ball is *not* moving with constant speed; let's say it's lying on the left-hand side in the beginning and then accelerated with a constant acceleration. This is the so-called quadratic easing and is displayed in the following figure. We can see that the position changes quadratically over time:

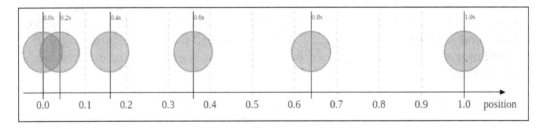

This effect is also visible in the easing function in the next figure. We can see that instead of a straight line of the linear easing, the function of quadratic easing is nonlinear. In D3.js, we can use the built-in d3.ease('quad') easing function to create a transition with quadratic easing.

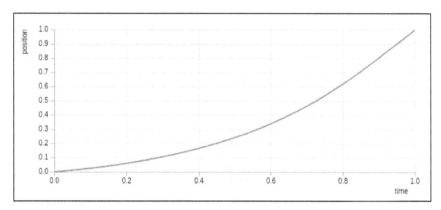

Quadratic easing function

If we want to model an animation with an increasing acceleration, we can use the cubic easing function d3.ease('cubic'), which we can see in the following figure. Now, the position values increase by the power of three for every interval:

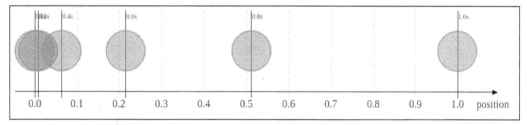

We can see the slightly steeper cubic easing function in the next figure:

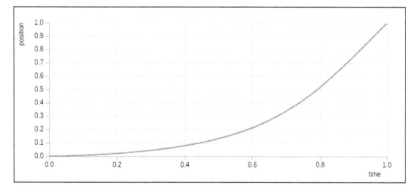

Cubic easing function

In general, we are free to design any easing function that we want in order to create custom easing effects. For example, let's take the slope of a sine function as an easing function:

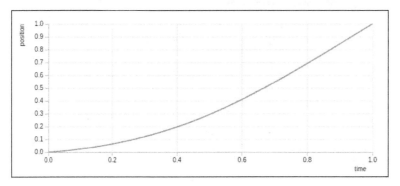

Sine easing function

The transition of the ball using the preceding easing function looks like the following figure:

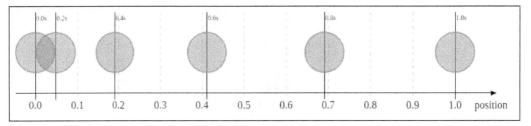

We can use any easing that we want if we can design an appropriate easing function. All the previous examples can be easily created with cubic Bézier curves, but this is not really a constraint. We can also use much more complex functions to model bouncing or elastic materials if we can describe it with a parametric equation.

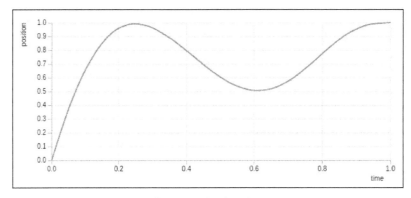

Custom easing function

In general, we will use the built-in d3.ease() function or design the animations with the control points of Bézier curves (this is also possible in CSS transitions). In all other cases, we will probably use easing functions that some very clever people already wrote for us.

 You can find very useful information about easing functions and many implementations for the Web in CSS and JavaScript at http://easings.net/.

Transitions in charts

In this section, we will apply the knowledge of the discussed sections on animations and transitions to the charts that we designed in the previous chapters.

To create a basic enter animation for a bar chart—like the one that we can see in the following figure—we need to first create a transition for the position of each bar on the y axis and the height of each bar:

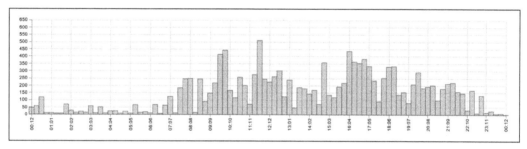

The bar chart

We want to animate from the position of the 0 value to the y value of the data point. Let's write this down as follows:

```
svg.select('.data')
  .selectAll('rect').data(data)
  .attr('r', 2.5)
  .attr('x', function(d) { return xScale(d.x) - barWidth*0.5; })
  .attr('width', function(d) { return barWidth; })
  .attr('y', yScale(0))
  .attr('height', 0)
  .transition()
  .attr('y', function(d) { return yScale(d.y); })
  .attr('height', function(d) { return yScale(0) -
    yScale(d.y); });
```

This is the most basic enter transition that we can think of because we are animating solely along the *y* axis with the same duration for every data point. We can see a schematic of the animation in the following figure:

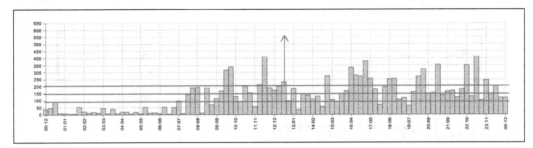

Linear transition along the y axis

If the duration of the animation of every data point should depend on its y value, we need to add a relative duration:

```
var max = d3.max(data, function(d){ return d.y; });
var duration = 2500;

svg.select('.data')
  .selectAll('rect').data(data)
  .attr('r', 2.5)
  .attr('x', function(d) { return xScale(d.x) - barWidth*0.5; })
  .attr('width', function(d) { return barWidth; })
  .attr('y', yScale(0))
  .attr('height', 0)
  .transition()
  .duration(function(d, i){ return duration*(d.y/max); })
  .attr('y', function(d) { return yScale(d.y); })
  .attr('height', function(d) { return yScale(0) -
    yScale(d.y); });
```

Now, as we can see in the following figure, the duration for small y values is shorter than for big ones and the maximum y value will have the maximum duration of the animation:

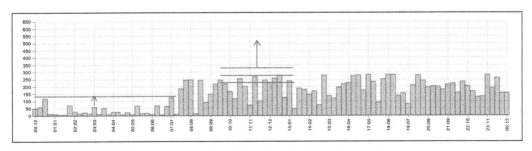

Linear transition with varying durations along y axis

To make the animation slightly more realistic, we add a cubic easing function:

```
var max = d3.max(data, function(d){ return d.y; });
var duration = 2500;

svg.select('.data')
  .selectAll('rect').data(data)
  .attr('r', 2.5)
  .attr('x', function(d) { return xScale(d.x) - barWidth*0.5; })
  .attr('width', function(d) { return barWidth; })
  .attr('y', yScale(0))
  .attr('height', 0)
  .transition()
  .duration(function(d, i){ return duration*(d.y/max); })
  .ease('cubic')
  .attr('y', function(d) { return yScale(d.y); })
  .attr('height', function(d) { return yScale(0) -
    yScale(d.y); });
```

We can see in the following figure that the animation is not linear anymore, but cubic along the *y* axis:

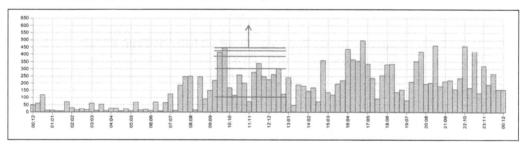

Cubic transition with varying durations along the y axis

Now, the animation along the *y* axis looks great, but all the values are animated at the same time. In the next step, we stagger the transitions along the *x* axis by enabling a delay for every element:

```
var max = d3.max(data, function(d){ return d.y; });
var duration = 2500;

svg.select('.data')
  .selectAll('rect').data(data)
  .attr('r', 2.5)
  .attr('x', function(d) { return xScale(d.x) - barWidth*0.5; })
  .attr('width', function(d) { return barWidth; })
  .attr('y', yScale(0))
```

```
.attr('height', 0)
.transition()
.duration(function(d, i){ return duration*(d.y/max); })
.delay(function(d,i) { return 100*i; })
.ease('cubic')
.attr('y', function(d) { return yScale(d.y); })
.attr('height', function(d) { return yScale(0) -
  yScale(d.y); });
```

In the following figure, we see the output of the preceding code. The chart is now created from left to right and it's very easy to follow how the data gets appended to the visualization:

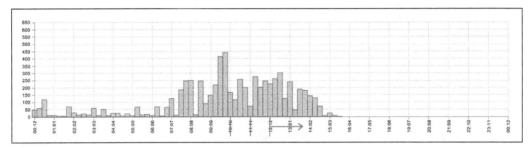

Linear transition along the x axis

To also make this animation along the *x* axis more realistic, we can add easing to the time staggering delay of the animation. To achieve this, we need to create an easing function and use it depending on the x position of the chart. Let's take a look at the code:

```
var easing = d3.ease('cubic');
var max = d3.max(data, function(d){ return d.y; });
var duration = 2500;

svg.select('.data')
  .selectAll('rect').data(data)
  .attr('r', 2.5)
  .attr('x', function(d) { return xScale(d.x) - barWidth*0.5; })
  .attr('width', function(d) { return barWidth; })
  .attr('y', yScale(0))
  .attr('height', 0)
  .transition()
  .duration(function(d, i){ return duration*(d.y/max); })
  .ease('cubic')
  .delay(function(d,i) { return duration*easing
    ((i+1)/data.length); })
```

```
.attr('y', function(d) { return yScale(d.y); })
.attr('height', function(d) { return yScale(0) -
  yScale(d.y); });
```

First, we create a custom parametric `easing(t)` function, which we then apply on the `delay` property of every element. The `delay` element is computed using the `duration` time — the easing factor (between 0 and 1), which is defined by the `ith` position of the element, and the used easing method. Thus, the first element has a very short delay and the last element is delayed by the `duration` time. We see the nonlinear transition along the *x* axis in the output of the preceding code (see the following figure):

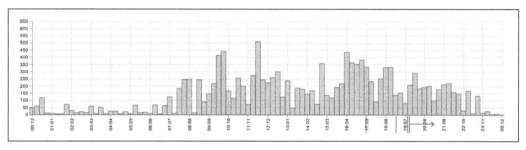

Cubic transition along the x axis

Summary

In this chapter, you learned the basics of animations in D3.js. You also learned that animations are timer triggered changes of properties. D3.js implements high performance timers and uses the native `requestAnimationFrame()` method if available.

Interpolators are parametric functions that return an interpolated value for a parameter between 0 and 1. D3.js integrates a variety of interpolation functions, but we can easily implement a new one for our data types. Transitions are much more comfortable and elegant than creating custom timers and interpolators. We also saw how to chain and stagger transitions and put them together piecewise to create animations.

After playing around with some examples of transitions, we discovered that there exist attributes that cannot be automatically interpolated. This concerns mainly the area and line generators that are used to generate the `d` attribute for path elements. Tweens are a way to implement custom interpolation functions for the transition of complex attributes and styles.

In the following section, we made the transition from linear animation step sizes to arbitrary step sizes with the use of easing functions. We also discussed physically realistic quadratic easing, cubic easing, and also bounce easing.

Finally, we applied all the theory about transitions, tweens, and easing to the previously designed chart types. We saw that we need to design all the enter, update, and exit transition separately.

In the following chapter, we will bring the charts to life and add interactions. We will learn how to use filters and brushes to control the datasets by interaction with the visualizations.

8
Bringing the Chart to Life with Interactions

In this chapter, we want to bring the chart to life and make the previous visualizations interactive. The biggest advantage of presenting data visualizations and graphs on the Web is that they can become interactive very easily. Interactive visualizations allow a much better understanding and processing of the data.

First, we will speak about events and event listeners in JavaScript in general. Then, we will focus on D3.js. This will enable us to understand how interactions are implemented on the lowest level and take this knowledge to implement a higher level control.

Then, we will directly use the event listeners to implement cursors for the previously developed chart directives. After a simple example, you will learn how to extract the nearest data point relative to the cursor position in order to implement snappy cursors.

In the following section, you will learn how to create custom events with D3.js in order to update the AngularJS scope from within the D3.js chart library. We will understand how proper encapsulation and event systems can facilitate the integration of our components.

After cursors, we will take a close look at zooming and panning. We will start with a simple zooming example. This example can be very useful in different applications. However, in a chart application, we would prefer a more functional zoom and panning (such as zooming on the time scale x axis). We will implement this as a second example. Later, we will come back to the AngularJS application-side to learn about filters and how they can be used in the application. We will then use the filter directly in the directive to implement a fully synchronous date range filter for all our chart directives.

Range filters for selecting ranges on the *x* axis are a common task in data visualizations; thus, D3.js implements a very flexible advanced filter for this job—so-called brushes. We will modify the range filter from the previous section and implement a similar filter with brushes in the last section. In this chapter, you will learn about native events and event listeners:

- Learn how to extract the nearest data point relative to the cursor position
- Implement a snappy cursor
- Implement labels
- Learn about custom events and event listeners
- Integrate an event system into the chart application
- Implement a simple zoom
- Implement an *x* axis zoom for time series
- Implement a date range filter and brushes

Listen for events

Interactions in JavaScript are based on the concept of events and event listeners. This concept works like this: first, one defines an event listener on an element. Then, it waits for a specific event of the element to occur, for example, this could be a click event. Every time the event occurs (the element is clicked on), a callback function is executed. Having said that, we can attach listeners to any element of the DOM and trigger functions as soon as the event occurs.

In D3.js, we can attach listeners directly to Selections via the .on(event, callback) method. Whenever D3.js handles an event, the d3.event variable stores all the information of the currently triggered event. Let's look at a simple example:

```
svg.on('click', function(){

  var e = d3.event;

  // Get relative cursor position
  var xpos = (e.offsetX==undefined) ? e.layerX : e.offsetX;
  var ypos = (e.offsetY==undefined) ? e.layerY : e.offsetY;

  svg.append("circle")
    .attr("cx", xpos)
    .attr("cy", ypos)
    .style("fill", "steelblue")
    .attr("r", 50);
});
```

In the preceding example, we attached a `click` listener to the `svg` node that generates a `circle` element with the center point coordinates of the current `click` event (actually, we use the offset coordinates, namely, `offsetX` and `offsetY` in Chrome and `layerX` and `layerY` in Firefox of the root `svg` node). The output of the example after a few clicks looks similar to the following figure:

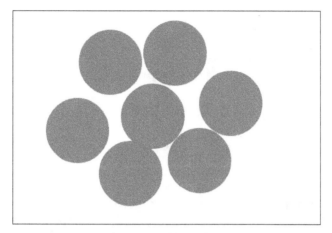

Circles generated by click events

Type of Events

Now, we know how listeners are attached to elements and callbacks are executed when a specific event occurs. In web visualizations, we will mostly use mouse events; thus, I will provide a list of the most common ones in their correct execution order (from top to bottom):

- `mouseenter`: This event occurs when the mouse cursor is entering the element
- `mouseover`: This event occurs when the mouse cursor is hovering over the element
- `mousemove`: This event occurs when the mouse is moved over the element
- `mousedown`: This event occurs when the mouse button is pressed
- `mouseup`: This event occurs when the mouse button is released
- `click`: This event occurs when the element is clicked on
- `dblclick`: This event occurs when the element is double-clicked
- `mouseleave`: This event occurs when the mouse cursor is leaving the element

 A complete list of DOM events and detailed explanations are available at `https://developer.mozilla.org/en-US/docs/Web/Events`.

Let's take a look at how these events are dispatched when they are assigned to an event handler. Therefore, we create an array of events and attach them to a `circle` node:

```
var circle = svg.append("circle")
  .attr("cx", 100)
  .attr("cy", 100)
  .attr("r", 50);

var events = [
  'click', 'dblclick',
  'mouseover', 'mouseenter', 'mouseleave',
  'mousemove', 'mousedown', 'mouseup'
];

events.map(function(e){
  circle.on(e, function(){
    console.log("Triggered", d3.event.type);
  });
});
```

In the preceding example, we use the `type` property on `d3.event` to obtain information on the type of event that was triggered. If we open the example in the browser and move the mouse over the circle to perform a double-click on it, we can see the order of the dispatched events in the console. The output should look similar to the following screenshot:

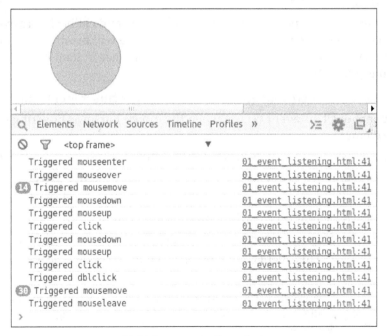

Multiple events are dispatched

Getting event coordinates

As we saw before, we have access to the current event in the event callback function with the d3.event object. This object gives us access to a variety of useful properties of the event, such as the position of the mouse cursor, the key code of a pressed key, or the time stamp of the event. Besides, the position of the cursor in global screen coordinates (screenX, screenY) and in local DOM coordinates (clientX, clientY), we also have access to the relative offset (offsetX, offsetY) to the element on which the event listener was called in Chrome. However, in Firefox, we need to use layerX and layerY to get the coordinates relative to the parent.

> More information on the *Event* object and detailed explanation of the attributes can be found at https://developer.mozilla.org/en-US/docs/Web/API/Event. You can find detailed information on the *MouseEvent* at https://developer.mozilla.org/en-US/docs/Web/API/MouseEvent.

More useful coordinates are provided by d3.mouse(container) and d3.touch(container), which return the position of the mouse or touches relative to a container element.

Let's see an example for this and implement a simple drawing tool:

```
var is_drawing = false;

svg.on('mousemove', function(){

  var pos = d3.mouse(this);

  if (is_drawing) {
    svg.append("circle")
      .attr("cx", pos[0])
      .attr("cy", pos[1])
      .style("fill", "red")
      .attr("r", 3);
  }
}).on('mousedown', function(){
  is_drawing = true;
}).on('mouseup', function(){
  is_drawing = false;
});
```

In the preceding example, we set is_drawing to true when we press the mouse button (mousedown) and we set this to false when we release the mouse button (mouseup). Once is_drawing is true, we obtain the position of the mouse relative to the current element (the svg node) by calling d3.mouse(this). Finally, we place a small circle on the current position of the cursor. The output of my drawing skills can be observed in the following screenshot:

Simple drawing application

Cursors

With the previous knowledge, we are already prepared to implement cursors for our visualization directives. Cursor lets us interact with the visualization because they can show us more detail about the presented values. In my opinion, every two-dimensional graph should have an option to enable cursors; it facilitates understanding a graph.

A simple cursor

First, we want to start with a cursor that solely follows the mouse movements and shows the current values of the axes at the position of the cursor. The following image visualizes what we want to achieve. I bordered the cursor values with red color to better show where we want to place the cursor labels later:

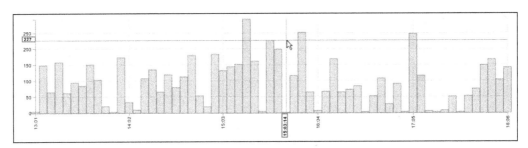

A simple cursor

First, let's discuss the steps that we have to implement to achieve a result similar to the previous image. Every time we move the mouse, we need to:

- Find the coordinates of the cursor
- Get the corresponding axis values of the cursor's coordinates
- Draw a line parallel to the *y* axis at the *x* position of the cursor
- Draw a line parallel to the *x* axis at the *y* position of the cursor
- Add a label of the *x* value at the *x* position of the cursor on the *x* axis
- Add a label of the *y* value at the *y* position of the cursor on the *y* axis

Okay, let's get started and add a cursor container and the lines and labels of the cursor to our bar chart directive. We will add these steps to the initialization of the chart to make sure the elements are created just once:

```
/* src/chart.js */
...
.directive('myBarChart', ["d3",
  function(d3){
    ...
    var cursorCont = axisCont.append('g').attr('class', 'cursor');
    cursorCont.append('line').attr('class', 'x-cursor cursor');
    cursorCont.append('line').attr('class', 'y-cursor cursor');
    cursorCont.append('text').attr('class', 'x-label label');
    cursorCont.append('text').attr('class', 'y-label label');
  }
])
```

Now, we can modify the `draw()` function where we actually draw the graph. We add an event listener for the `mousemove` event in order to compute the cursor position and values every time users move the mouse:

```
/* src/chart.js --> draw() */

...
.directive('myBarChart', ["d3",
  function(d3){
    function draw(...) {
      ...
      var xCursor = svg.select('.x-cursor');
      var yCursor = svg.select('.y-cursor');
      var xLabel = svg.select('.x-label');
      var yLabel = svg.select('.y-label');
      svg.on('mousemove', function(){
```

```
                // Implement fancy cursors here
            });
        }
    }
])
```

First, in the `mousemove` event handler, we need to get the cursor coordinates relative to the `svg` node and the corresponding axis values:

```
/* src/chart.js --> draw() */
...
svg.on('mousemove', function(){
    var pos = d3.mouse(this);
    var xValue = xScale.invert(pos[0]);
    var yValue = yScale.invert(pos[1]);
    var xMin = d3.min(data, function(d) { return d.x; });
    var xMax = d3.max(data, function(d) { return d.x; });
    var yMax = d3.max(data, function(d) { return d.y; });
});
```

In the preceding code, we use the scale `.invert()` method to obtain a valid dataset value from a given pixel value (this is discussed in more detail in *Chapter 3, Manipulating Data*). We also compute the maximum values of both *x* and *y* axis.

Finally, we can move the first line to the x position of the cursor and add the x value as a label rotated 90 degrees to the *x* axis. We also want to format the label such that it shows hours, minutes, and seconds and that the cursor can just move between the areas of the chart:

```
/* src/chart.js --> draw() */
...
svg.on('mousemove', function(){
...
    xCursor
        .attr('x1', pos[0])
        .attr('y1', yScale(0))
        .attr('x2', pos[0])
        .attr('y2', yScale(yMax));

    xLabel
        .attr('transform', 'translate('+pos[0]+','+(yMax + 8)+')
        rotate(-90)')
        .text(d3.time.format('%H:%I:%S')(+xValue));
});
```

Also, as a last step, we do the same for the second line of the cursor and the label on the *y* axis. The format of this label can be the same as the one we used previously for the ticks on the *y* axis:

```
/* src/chart.js --> draw() */
...
svg.on('mousemove', function(){
...
  yCursor
    .attr('x1', xScale(0))
    .attr('y1', pos[1])
    .attr('x2', xScale(xMax))
    .attr('y2', pos[1]);

  yLabel
    .attr('transform', 'translate('+(xScale(0)-8)+','+pos[1]+')')
    .text(d3.format('f')(yValue));
});
```

This wasn't very complicated, wasn't it? Let's make the cursor a little bit more helpful because right now this cursor just blindly follows the mouse cursor!

Snappy cursors

Although cursors help us to understand the data of a graph better, cursors that move completely aligned with the mouse coordinates do not show the most valuable information. In the next step, we want to implement cursors that automatically snap to the nearest data point from the cursor position; the following image visualizes our goal:

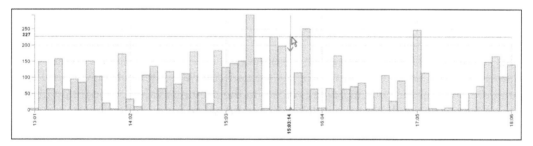

Explanation of a snappy cursor

To solve this particular problem, we have to add one more step (the third point in the following list) to the previous implementation:

- Find the coordinates of the cursor
- Get the corresponding axis values of the cursor's coordinates

- Get the nearest data point
- Draw a line parallel to the y axis at the x position of the nearest data point
- Draw a line parallel to the x axis at the y position of the nearest data point
- Add a label of the x value at the x position of the cursor on the x axis
- Add a label of the y value at the y position of the cursor on the y axis

In this implementation, I will only discuss the difference to the previous example—finding the nearest value in the dataset—and I will implement this cursor for the area chart. Let's start with getting the x-value of the current cursor position:

```
/* src/chart.js --> draw() */
...
svg.on('mousemove', function(){
  var pos = d3.mouse(this);
  var valueX = xScale.invert(pos[0]);
});
```

As a second step, we need to find the nearest data point. To do so, we will need to traverse the dataset and return the index of the element whose value is bigger than the provided value. In D3.js, this can be achieved by using the d3.bisector() function, in our case, custom bisectors and an accessor function for the x coordinate:

```
/* src/chart.js --> draw() */
...
svg.on('mousemove', function(){
  ...
  // Create a bisector with an accessor function
  // that traverses the array from left
  var xBisect = d3.bisector(function(d) { return d.x; }).left;
  // Apply the bisector
  var index = xBisect(data, xValue);
});
```

This is a really neat function because we don't need to implement the traversal ourselves! Now, we have the index of the element after the intersection; we need to compare whether the current value is closer to the previous value or the following one. We also check whether the index is in a valid range for our next steps:

```
/* src/chart.js --> draw() */
...
svg.on('mousemove', function(){
  ...
  if (index == 0 || index > data.length) {
    return;
  }
  var d0 = data[index - 1];
```

```
    var d1 = data[index];
    // get the nearest value
    var d = xValue - d0.x > d1.x - xValue ? d1 : d0;
});
```

In the preceding example, the d variable references the nearest data point that corresponds to the current mouse cursor position. This was already the hardest part of the problem The rest is similar to the previous example of simple cursors, while just swapping the cursor position with the position of the data point in the graph (xScale(d.x), yScale(d.y)). Once we implemented this and added a focus to the active element, the result will look similar to the following figure:

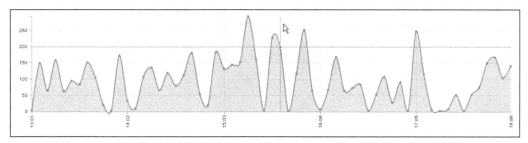

The snappy cursor in action

In the preceding image, we can see that the mouse cursor is above the data point and it's shifted slightly to the right-hand side along the *x* axis. However, the snappy cursor highlights the nearest data point on the *x* axis—just as we wanted.

Labeling the cursor position

Once we know the cursor position and its corresponding values on the axes, it's fairly easy to display labels that show the current cursor values. We want to display these labels as an overlay on the chart axis at the same position as the axis tick values. The label should have a label icon and contain the current value of the cursor on the corresponding axis.

First, we need to create a group that contains the label icon and the label text. We need to style the icon according to our needs. Note that in the previous example, we solely create a label text node, whereas now we will create a g node with a path node and text node inside. As we did previously with the cursor, we create the label once and later just move it to the current cursor position. Let's create all the elements in the chart initialization of the line chart directive:

```
/* src/chart.js */
...
.directive('myBarChart', ["d3",
  function(d3){
```

```
. . .
var xLabelNode = focusCont.append('g').attr('class', 'x-label
label');
var yLabelNode = focusCont.append('g').attr('class', 'y-label
label');

// Path for the label shape
var tag_path = 'M 51.166,23.963 62.359,17.5 c 1.43,-0.824
1.43,-2.175 0,-3 L 51.166,8.037 48.568,1.537 2,1.4693227
2,30.576466 48.568,30.463 z';

xLabelNode.append('path')
  .style('display', 'none')
  .attr('d', tag_path)
  .attr('transform', 'translate(-30, -15) scale(0.7)');
xLabelNode.append('text')
  .attr('transform', 'translate(-20)');

yLabelNode.append('path')
  .style('display', 'none')
  .attr('d', tag_path)
  .attr('transform', 'translate(-30, -15) scale(0.7)');
yLabelNode.append('text')
  .attr('transform', 'translate(-20)');
}])
```

In the preceding code, we add the label groups to `focusCont` — the container that shows all focus elements on the top of the chart. Thanks to this, the labels will be overlaying the axis ticks.

Now, we can implement the labels and move them to the corresponding position on the axis when the cursor moves. Let's define some margins and translate the label groups to their corresponding positions:

```
/* src/chart.js --> draw() */
. . .
svg.on('mousemove', function(){
. . .
  var xMargin = -8, yMargin = 3;

  var xLeft = xScale(d.x) + xMargin;
  var xTop = yScale(0);

  xLabel
    .transition()
```

```
    .ease(easing)
    .duration(duration)
    .attr('transform', 'translate('+xLeft+','+xTop+') rotate(-
    90)');

  var yLeft = xScale(xMin);
  var yTop = yScale(d.y) + yMargin;

  yLabel
    .transition()
    .ease(easing)
    .duration(duration)
    .attr('transform', 'translate('+yLeft+','+yTop+')');
});
```

Now, we need to display the label and update the values of the labels. So, we extend the preceding function by the following code:

```
/* src/chart.js --> draw() */
...
svg.on('mousemove', function(){
...
  xLabel.select('text')
    .text(d3.time.format('%H:%M')(+d.x));

  xLabel.select('path')
    .style('display', 'block');

  yLabel.select('text')
    .text(d3.format('f')(d.y));

  yLabelNode.select('path')
    .style('display', 'block');
});
```

In the preceding code, we use the same formatting functions that we used previously in the axis.

Now, if we look at the result of the cursor with the new labels, we see a chart similar to following figure:

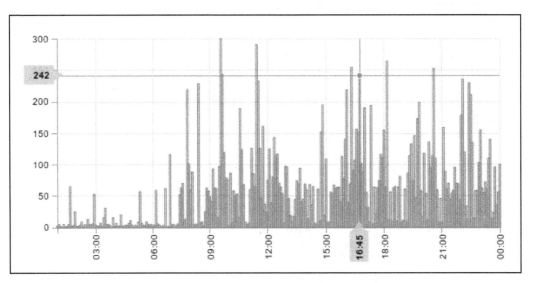

Snappy cursor with labels updating the AngularJS scope from D3.js

As a next step, we want to use the cursor data within the whole AngularJS application to display the current cursor position in another part of the application. This means that we need to somehow update the variables in the scope of the directive from within the chart library.

The first idea that comes to mind is to simply store the scope for each chart while initializing it, similar to the following example:

```
/* src/chart.js --> AngularJS directive  */
...
link: function(scope, element, attrs) {
  var chart = new Chart(element[0], scope);
  ...
}

/* src/chart.js --> D3.js chart library */
...
redraw: function() {
  ...
  this.scope.xCursor = xCurrent;
  ...
}
```

In the preceding code, we see that we could just call `scope.xCursor`, and so on to update variables on the scope from within the chart library. This technique might work as expected for a quick and dirty example, but it's a very bad integration; we just created a hard-coded dependency on AngularJS. If we want to use the chart library with any other JavaScript application framework in the future, we will have to rewrite and adapt the library for this framework.

The proper way to integrate the chart library and the application is to use an event system with event registrations and an event handler function. With this technique, we can listen for certain events—such as change of the cursor position—and update the scope outside the chart library. Thus, the chart library will not have to be adapted for any other frameworks. Let's see how the following example looks with the use of events:

```
/* src/chart.js --> AngularJS directive */
...
link: function(scope, element, attrs) {
  var chart = new Chart(element[0]);

  chart.on('cursorchange', function(xCurrent){
    scope.$apply(function() {
      scope.xCursor = xCurrent;
    });
  });
}
```

In the preceding example, we can see that now we have all the AngularJS relevant code inside the directive—only by encapsulating both services (the AngularJS directive and the D3.js library) and using an event system. With the `.on()` method, we will create an event listener for the `cursorchange` event and set the scope variable in the event handler. We need to wrap the code in the `scope.$apply()` block to trigger a digest after its execution and inform AngularJS about the changes. Let's take a look at how we can implement such an `.on()` function and integrate custom events into our chart library.

 Events and encapsulation are the cleanest and most robust way of integrating services.

Customizing events in D3.js

Fortunately, D3.js provides a solid and simple event system. This is also used by D3.js internally. To implement custom events, we need to first initialize an event, then register an event listener, and finally dispatch the event:

- `d3.dispatch(event)`: This initializes an event and creates a dispatcher
- `dispatch.on(event, listener)`: This registers an event handler
- `dispatch.event(args)`: This dispatches the event and calls all registered handlers

Let's look at an example where we want to listen for a `customevent`:

```
// Create dispatcher
var dispatch = d3.dispatch("customevent");

// Register handler
dispatch.on("customevent", function(args){

  console.log("Custom event called with", args);
});

// Disatch event
dispatch.customevent('some args');
```

If we run this example and look at the JavaScript console, we see the `Custom event called some args` expected output. In the preceding example, we also see how easy it is to use events in your D3.js library, so there is no excuse not to use it!

Displaying self-updating cursor values

Finally, we want to use the custom event system to implement a box that displays the custom cursor position. We will simply store the cursor position on the scope of the directive and bind it to a `span` tag below the chart. Then, we will update the scope variable with the new event system.

First, we need to set up and integrate the event system into the chart library. Then, we need to provide an `.on()` method on the chart object in order to register events. Let's get started; we will implement this in the initialization of the chart:

```
/* src/chart.js */
...
.directive('myBarChart', ["d3",
  function(d3){     ...
    // Initialize the 'cursorchange' event
    var dispatch = d3.dispatch("cursorchange");
  }
])
```

In the preceding example, we initialize the `cursorchange` event and make the event listener available directly on the `dispatch` variable. Now, we also need to make the dispatch variable available inside the `draw()` function; therefore, we add it as a `draw(..., dispatch)` argument. As a next step, we need to call the event dispatcher when the cursor position changes (the mouse moves over the chart):

```
/* src/chart.js --> draw() */
...
svg.on('mousemove', function(){

  ...
  // dispatch all cursor change events
  dispatch.cursorchange([d.x, d.y]);
});
```

In the end, we dispatch the `cursorchange` event with the current cursor values as arguments.

Now, we can implement the event listener in the directive—exactly as we saw in the integration example in the beginning of this section. Don't forget to add the `cursor` variable to the private scope of the directive:

```
/* src/chart.js   */
...
scope: {
  data: '=',
  cursor: '='
},
link: function(scope, element, attrs) {
  ...
  /* Listen on cursor change */
  dispatch.on('cursorchange', function(cursor) {
```

```
        if (cursor){
          scope.$apply(function() {
            scope.cursor = cursor;
          });
        }
    });
    ...
}
```

In the preceding example, we can see that custom events work exactly as they should by simply registering a listener on the dispatch variable with the .on(event, listener) method. Now, let's add the cursor to the main controller of the application:

```
/* src/app.js */
...
// Main application controller
.controller('MainCtrl', ["$scope", ...
  function ($scope, ...) {

    $scope.display = {
      cursor: []
    };
    ...
  }
]);
```

Finally, we can display the cursor variables in the application:

```
<!-- index.html -->
<div>
  <span>Cursor:</span>
  <span>
    {{ display.cursor[0] | date : 'dd.MM.yyyy HH:mm' }}
  </span>
  <span>
    {{ display.cursor[1] | number:2 }}
  </span>
</div>
<bar-chart class="chart" data="log.data"
cursor="display.cursor"></bar-chart>
```

In the preceding code snippet, we bind the `display.cursor` object from the scope of the controller to the private scope of the directive. This automatically updates the cursor value in the controller for us. Then, we display both values with a date filter for the x value and a number filter for the y value. We can see the result of this implementation in the following image:

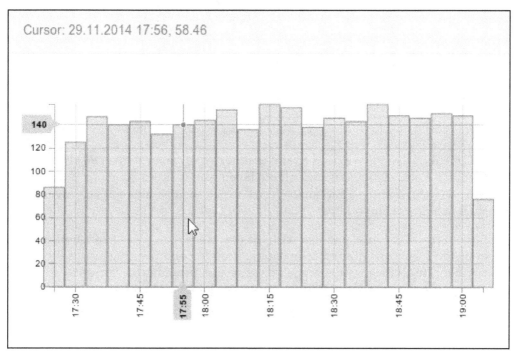

Chart with self-updating cursor values

Zooming and panning

We will very soon encounter a problem that some differences between two neighboring data points are very small and hard to grasp. In this case, it will be very handy to just zoom in to this particular position.

A simple zoom

Let's start with a simple example of a zoom where we just want to enlarge the viewpoint of the svg image. The following figure illustrates the problem:

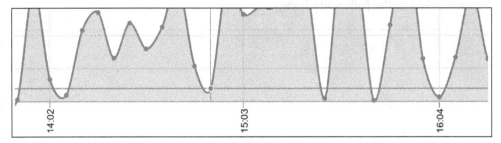

Zoomed viewpoint of the chart

To implement this zoom, we need to add another group layer to the svg element, which contains all the previous underlying layers and handles zooming and panning properly via the translate and scale transformation attributes so that we don't have to touch other components.

Then, zooming can be implemented with the d3.behavior.zoom() function, a helper method that can automatically handle zooming and panning events for mouse and touch inputs. If the event is triggered, d3.event provides the current scale and translation values to zoom and pan. Let's add this behavior to the area chart:

```
/* src/chart.js --> draw() */
...
var translateZ = [0,0];
var scaleZ = 1;
var zoom = d3.behavior.zoom()
    .on("zoom", function() {
  translateZ = d3.event.translate;
  scaleZ = d3.event.scale;
  svg.select('.vis')
  .attr("transform", "translate(" + translateZ + ")scale(" +
  scaleZ + ")");
    });
```

Now, we just need to call the zoom function on the element that listens for the zoom event. In our case, this element will be the root svg node; thus, we write the following code:

```
svg.call(zoom);
```

This is already the solution to the simple zooming problem. However, we want a better zooming experience, so let's zoom the chart just along the *x* axis.

An x axis zoom

The simple zoom example is a nice gimmick, but not really helpful in a real visualization application. More likely, we want to zoom the data area of the graph and update the axis accordingly. This is exactly what we want to implement now for the *x* axis.

This is again done with the use of d3.behavior.zoom() and it's nearly completely automatic. The reason for this is that we can attach a scale object to the zoom object, which adapts the domain of the scale automatically for us according to the current zoom and pan. The only thing left to do is to update the data points and the axis. Let's take a look at the implementation directly in our chart library:

```
/* src/chart.js --> draw() */
...
var zoom = d3.behavior.zoom()
  .x(xScale)
  .on("zoom", function() {

    // Update x-Axis
    svg.select('.x-axis').call(xAxis);
    svg.select('.x-grid').call(xGrid);

    // Update data points
    svg.select('.data')
    .selectAll('circle').data(data)
    .attr('cx', function(d) { return xScale(d.x); })
    .attr('cy', function(d) { return yScale(d.y); });

    // line1 contains the line generator
    svg.select(".data-line").attr('d', line1);
    // area1 contains the area generator
    svg.select(".data-area").attr('d', area1);
  });

svg.call(zoom);
```

As we see in the preceding example, simply attaching the scale object to the zoom function magically does all the zooming and panning actions. We can see the output of the *x* axis zoom in the following image:

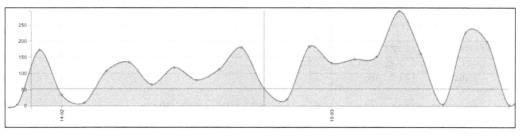

Zoom on x axis

Interactive filters

Let's switch back to AngularJS for a section. To be precise, let's take a look at filters. Let's implement two filters that compare Date objects and returns the elements of an array that are greater than or equal to a specific date (gte_date) and less than or equal to a specific date (lte_d). First, we need to add a filter via the .filter(name, filter_func) function to the AngularJS chart component. The filter_func argument needs to return a function in the shape of function(arg1, arg2, ...), where arg1 is usually the input array that finally returns the filtered array. Okay, let's implement this:

```
/* src/chart.js */
.filter('gte_date', function(){
  return function(input, raw_date){
    var date = new Date(raw_date);
    return isNaN(date.getTime()) ? input :
    input.filter(function(d){
      return d.x >= date;
    });
  };
})

.filter('lte_date', function(){
  return function(input, raw_date){
    var date = new Date(raw_date);
    return isNaN(date.getTime()) ? input :
    input.filter(function(d){
      return d.x <= date;
    });
  };
})
```

In the preceding code, we added a check if the provided raw_date parameter generates a valid Date object. If so, we apply the filter and if not, we return the input unfiltered. We can now use this filter directly in the directive template, as shown in the following code snippet:

```
/* src/app.js */
...
// Main application controller
.controller('MainCtrl', ["$scope", ...
  function ($scope, ...) {

    $scope.startDate = '2014-11-26T12:00:00+0100';
    $scope.endDate = '2014-11-26T17:00:00+0100';
    ...
```

```
    }]);
```

```html
<!-- index.html -->
<my-line-chart data="log.data | gte_date:startDate |
lte_date:endDate"></my-line-chart>
```

For our application, another approach is more interesting. We want to share the
selected start and ending dates throughout the whole AngularJS application and in
D3.js as well. Therefore, it's better to define `startDate` and `endDate` as attributes for
the directive so that we can modify them from within the visualization; let's adapt
the directive in such a way that it links both attributes on scope:

```
/* src/chart.js  */
...scope: {
  data: '=',
  cursor: '=',
  startDate: '=',
  endDate: '='
},
...
```

The HTML template of the directive also needs to be adapted as follows:

```html
<my-line-chart data="data" start-date="startDate" end-
date="endDate"></my-line-chart>
```

The previous changes imply that we now need to apply the previously implemented
filters in the directive. An AngularJS filter can be called outside the HTML template
with the `$filter('name')(arg1, arg2, ...)` syntax. Let's inject the `$filter`
module to the bar chart directive and add a `filter()` function to the directive:

```
/* src/chart.js */
...// Bar Chart directive
.directive('myBarChart', ["d3", "$filter",
  function(d3, $filter){
    ...
    function filter(data, minDate, maxDate) {
      // Create a new array
      var d = data.slice(0);
      if (minDate !== undefined) {
        d = $filter('gte_date')(d, minDate);
      }
      if (maxDate !== undefined) {
        d = $filter('lte_date')(d, maxDate);
      }
      return d;
    }
    ...
  }])
```

Now, we can simply call this new `filter()` function in the `link` function of the chart directive to filter the dataset and extract the data between `minDate` and `maxDate`:

```
/* src/chart.js --> link() */
...
// Watch the data attribute of the scope
scope.$watch('[data, startDate, endDate]', function(newVal, oldVal,
scope) {

  // Update the chart
  if (scope.data) {
    var data = filter(scope.data, scope.startDate, scope.endDate);
    draw(svg, width, height, data, dispatch);
  }
}, true);
...
```

I want to quickly summarize what the last changes enabled us to do. It allows you to keep the starting and ending dates of the date filter inside the `app` controller and link them to all time series directives. This means that we can filter all charts in our visualization at the same time with a simple date filter. That's awesome.

To make the filter visually more appealing, we can add an AngularJS Bootstrap date range picker (see the following image) to select the period of interest more easily:

AngularJS Bootstrap date range picker

However, we should also somehow consider that the `DateTime` input for the date filter accepts time as an input, so we should also provide this as a Selection method. Moreover, a better way will be to use the native HTML5 input elements for date and time to define the starting and ending point for the filter. If we implement this, the result looks similar to the following figure:

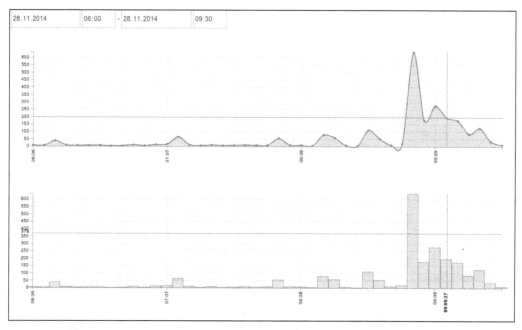

Date and time filters

Advanced filtering using brushes

In the previous section, we saw that D3.js can handle all the filtering action with solely modifying the domain and range attributes of the axis object. Filtering and selecting data is a common task in data visualization; therefore, D3.js implements a much more advanced filtering method called brushes.

A brush is a D3.js module initialized with an *x* and/or a *y* axis scale and automatically creates a draggable and resizeable box on top of a visualization container. While dragging and resizing this box, the brush automatically adapts the range and domain of the axis scales. A brush often looks similar to the following image:

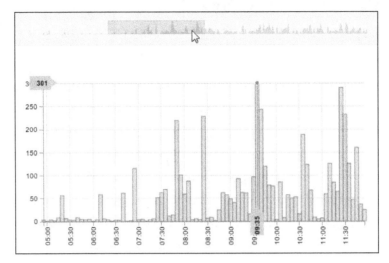

Filtering time scale axis with a brush

This brush looks really cool as a filter; we also want to implement such a brush for the start and end date filter of the application. The goal is to build a very simple area chart in the navigation bar that shows the data of the first chart. This chart should serve as a graphical date filter, where we can move the box of the brush and automatically filter all charts in our application. We also want to create a new directive for this, so we can easily test and reuse it.

Creating a simple brush

First, let's take a look at brushes in D3.js and how to initialize and use them. A simple brush object can be created by the d3.svg.brush() function. Afterward, we can set the scales for the axes with the .x(scale) and/or .y(scale) methods. Finally, we can draw the brush controls in a Selection with selection.call(brush).

We start with implementing a container for the visualization that will contain our simple brush:

```
var width = 800, height = 200, margin = 15;

var svg = d3.select("body").append("svg")
  .attr("width", width)
  .attr("height", height);
```

Next, we create a scale for the data with the range of visualization container; we will solely use the *x* axis for this simple example and an arbitrary range from 0 to 10:

```
var xScale = d3.scale.linear()
    .range([margin, width-margin])
    .domain([0, 10]);
```

Let's display an axis for this scale:

```
var axis = d3.svg.axis()
    .scale(xScale)
    .orient('top');

var axisContainer = svg.append("g")
    .attr("class", "axis")
    .attr("transform", "translate(0, "+(height-margin)+")")
    .call(axis);
```

The result of the preceding example shows a simple axis at the bottom of the chart (see the following image). When we move the mouse over the chart, we see the standard mouse cursor. This is the default cursor, meaning that currently no interaction is possible:

Simple container with axis

Now, we can create a new brush based on our scale and add the brush container to the chart. In order to use the brush for a single axis, we need to scale the brush elements to the fixed height of the visualization area:

```
var brush = d3.svg.brush()
    .x(xScale);

var brushContainer = svg.append("g")
    .attr("class", "brush")
    .call(brush);

brushContainer.selectAll("rect")
    .attr("y", 0)
    .attr("height", height);
```

Let's look at the result and move the cursor over the chart area (see the top portion of the following image); we see a crosshair cursor symbol that indicates a possible interaction. The cursor is autogenerated by the D3.js brush and enables the user to draw a box in the chart area.

When we look at the DOM tree (see the bottom portion of the following figure), we see the generated brush group that contains a `rect` background (which enables the crosshair cursor), a `rect` extent (which enables to move the cursor and shows the current brush range), and two more `resize` groups (which enable the resize cursor and enables horizontal resizing of the current brush range):

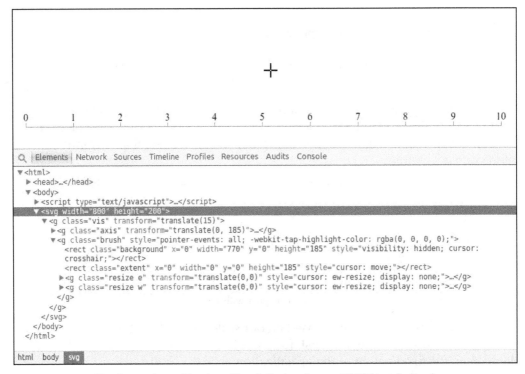

Simple container with axis and brush (top) and current DOM tree (bottom)

Let's add a little style to the visualization:

```css
<style type="text/css">
.brush .extent {
  stroke: rgba(255, 185, 88, 0.9);
  fill-opacity: .125;
  shape-rendering: crispEdges;
}
</style>
```

If we now start to draw a rectangle on the brush area while holding the left mouse button, we can see the extent rectangle appearing in light gray on the chart surface (see the following image):

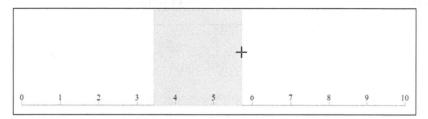

Simple container with brush and active extent

Finally, we want to do something with the chart after drawing an extent area with the brush. To have full control over the interaction, D3.js provides three events for brush interactions:

- `brushstart`: This event gets fired when we start brushing
- `brush`:This event gets fired while we are brushing
- `brushend`: This event gets fired after we stop brushing

The current extent can be simply retrieved by calling the `.extent()` method on the `brush` object. Let's extend the example so that the axis resizes automatically with the brush extent. We should not forget to clear the extent after resizing the axis. This can be achieved by executing `(brush.clear())(selection)` on the brush selection or the equivalent `selection.call(brush.clear())` function:

```
brush.on('brushend', function(){

    // Use the current extent
    xScale.domain(brush.extent());

    // Redraw the axis
    axisContainer
        .transition()
        .duration(250)
        .call(axis);

    // Clear the brush
    brushContainer.call(brush.clear());
});
```

In the preceding code, we animated the changes of the axis scale with a transition after the brush extent has changed. In the end, we clear the brush extent. The result of this brush can be seen in the following image, where the extent is selected at the top and the axis changed to the new scale at the bottom:

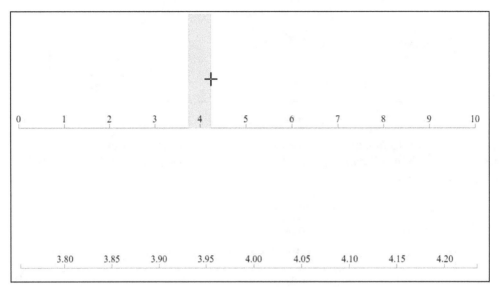

Modifying the axis scale with a brush while changing extent (top) and after changing extent (bottom)

Building a custom date filter directive

We will use the previously learned technique to create a date filter directive that previews a little area chart and lets us select a certain date range for the application. This means that we need to implement a new chart type for the brush and create a directive of it; let's get started. We implement a directive that is almost equal to the line chart directive; we solely add the brush container and brush event handlers:

```
/* src/chart.js */
...
// Brush Chart directive
.directive('myBrushChart', ["d3",
  function(d3){
    function draw(svg, width, height, data, dispatch) {
      ...
    }

    return {
      restrict: 'E',
      scope: {
        data: '='
```

```
          },
        compile: function( element, attrs, transclude ) {
          // Create a SVG root element
          var svg = d3.select(element[0]).append('svg');

          /* Create container */
          var visCont = svg.append('g').attr('class', 'vis');
          var dataCont = visCont.append('g').attr('class', 'data');
          var brushCont = visCont.append('g').attr('class', 'brush');

          dataCont.append('path').attr('class', 'data-line');
          dataCont.append('path').attr('class', 'data-area');

          // Initialize the brush events
          var dispatch = d3.dispatch(
            "brushstart", "brush", "brushend"
          );

          // Define the dimensions for the chart
          var width = 200, height = 50;

          // Return the link function
          return function(scope, element, attrs) {

            // Watch the data attribute of the scope
            scope.$watch('data', function(newVal, oldVal, scope) {

              // Update the chart
              if (scope.data) {
                draw(svg, width, height, scope.data, dispatch);
              }
            }, true);
          };
        }
      };
  }])
```

Now, we implement the brush in the `draw()` function to draw the brush area onto the Selection of the brush container. This is very similar to what you learned in the previous section about brushes:

```
/* src/chart.js --> draw() */...
var brush = d3.svg.brush()
  .x(xScale)
  .on('brushstart', function(){
```

```
        dispatch.brushstart(brush);
    })
    .on('brush', function(){
        dispatch.brush(brush);
    })
    .on('brushend', function(){
        dispatch.brushend(brush);
    });

svg.select('.brush')
    .call(brush)
    .selectAll("rect")
    .attr("y", 0)
    .attr("height", height-margin);
```

Let's look at the result of the preceding directive:

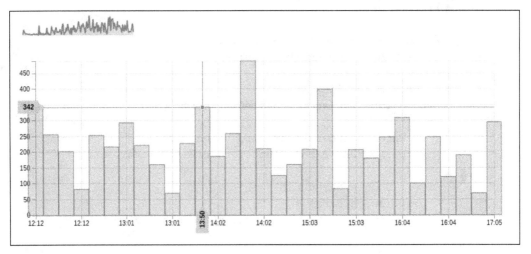

Brush directive as filter

Finally, we will append an event listener for the brush event. Every time the brush changes, we will write the extent to the brush variable on the scope. In the template, we will finally connect the brush variable with the date filter of the other charts:

```
/* src/chart.js */
...
// Brush Chart directive
.directive('myBrushChart', ["d3",
    function(d3){
    ...
        return {
```

```
      restrict: 'E',
      scope: {
         ...
         brush: '='
      },
      compile: function( element, attrs, transclude ) {
         ...
         dispatch.on('brush', function(brush){

           scope.$apply(function(){
             scope.brush = brush.extent();
           });
         });
      }
    }
  }
]);
```

Now, we can place the directive in the navigation bar. Voila! We have an awesome date filter that displays the area chart of the first dataset of the controller. We need to link the start-date and end-date attributes with the brush attribute:

```
<!-- index.html -->
...
<my-brush-chart class="chart" brush="display.date"
data="log.data"></my-brush-chart>
<my-bar-chart class="chart blue" data="log.data"
cursor="display.cursor" start-date="display.date[0]" end-
date="display.date[1]">
```

If we look at the resulting page, we can see that the custom filter looks very good in the navigation bar. The preview of the first dataset as an area chart is also helpful when selecting a certain time span:

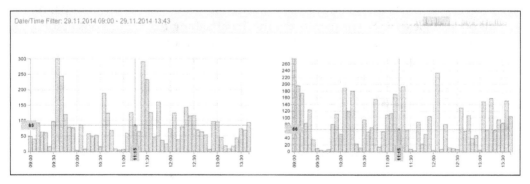

Brush directive as date filter

Summary

In this chapter, you learned various interaction techniques to enhance the usability of charts and to make them fully accessible.

First, we saw the concept of event listeners and events in JavaScript and how they are used with D3.js. We used the `.on(event, callback)` method to attach event callbacks directly on selection of elements. All the details about the triggered event are available in the `d3.event` object. When dealing with relative coordinates, the `d3.mouse(container)` function becomes quite handy because it returns the mouse coordinates relative to the container.

Then, we implemented a simple cursor for the chart directive that strictly follows the mouse position. We can easily compute the values on the axis by using the `scale.invert()` method. In the second cursor implementation, we also needed to compute the nearest value of the dataset to our current position on the axis. To achieve this, we used the `d3.bisector()` method with an accessor for the x value of the dataset values.

In the following section, we implemented floating labels for cursors. We realized that once the cursor position and axis values are known, drawing labels is very simple. Like the cursors, the labels are drawn once and moved to their corresponding position thereafter.

After understanding the concept of events and listeners and after using native events, we understood that event systems help us to encapsulate and integrate services. Therefore, we use the internal event system of D3.js to enable custom events for our chart, for example, the `cursorchange` event. Later in the directive, we can simply listen for this event and adapt the scope variables directly inside the directives. This enables a clear separation of the D3.js chart library and the AngularJS application.

Next, we looked at zooming and panning. In the first simple example, we used `d3.behavior.zoom()` to simply zoom the whole graphic. The second example was more important for data visualizations because it showed the zooming and panning actions on a single axis. We implemented this by attaching the `xScale` object for the axis scale to the `zoom` object. D3.js handles all translation and scaling operations automatically in the `domain` property of the scale object.

In the next chapter, we will put all the pieces together and finally create a dashboard to visualize real-time server logs.

9
Building a Real-time Visualization to Monitor Server Logs

In previous chapters, you learned different ways to load, process, and visualize data in the browser. In this chapter, we want to use all this knowledge to build an application that lets us monitor and visualize server logs in real time. If we think about a typical client-server approach, our application is divided into two parts: a web server that monitors log files and a client that interprets and visualizes these logs.

In the first section of this chapter, we will set up a Node.js server with the Express framework and use the built-in file system tools to monitor log files. We will propagate file changes in real time to the client with the use of a bidirectional WebSocket connection; we will use the *Socket.IO* library for this.

In the second section, we will implement and construct the client for the application whose job is to organize, process, and visualize the log data. We will also use Socket. IO on the client to load data from the bidirectional WebSocket connection. Finally, we will set up the log data and create custom parsers and processors for different styles of log files.

In this chapter, you will:

- Implement a static file server with Node.js, npm, and Express
- Implement real-time server push with Socket.IO
- Learn how to read and monitor files with Node.js
- Set up a simple web client with Bootstrap
- Learn how to use Socket.IO on the client with AngularJS

- Create custom parsers for different log types
- Be very happy for everything you achieved

Building a real-time monitoring server

In this section, we implement the server application. This application should be able to monitor files and communicate with multiple clients at the same time. These are the perfect requirements to use an event-driven, nonblocking I/O application platform such as Node.js. The fact that we can also code the server application in JavaScript is another huge advantage. Additionally, the built-in package manager npm provides a variety of useful and easy to use packages.

Setting up a Node.js application

First, we need to install Node.js on our development machine. We can download and install the latest binaries from http://nodejs.org/. Node.js automatically installs its npm package manager, which we will use to install all the required packages for the server application.

To create a Node.js application, we will first create a package.json file, a file that contains all metainformation about the application (such as name, version number, and dependencies):

```
{
    "name": "webserver-monitor",
    "version": "0.0.1",
    "description": "Webserver Monitor Application",
    "dependencies": {
    }
}
```

For now, we leave the dependencies section empty and add the dependencies automatically when we install packages via npm and the --save flag.

Setting up a web server that serves static files

In this book, we will use the excellent Node.js web framework *Express* and the serve-static package to kick off a web server in under 10 lines of code. I will not go into the details about Express, but we will see that it's very easy and straightforward to use for our purpose.

So, let's add both the packages to our application. To do so, we open the terminal in the root directory of the project and execute the following commands in the terminal:

```
npm install --save express
npm install --save serve-static
```

These commands will add both the packages and their current versions as dependencies to the `package.json` file and download and install them in the `npm_packages` directory. The native Node.js function `require()`, which imports packages and modules, will automatically look for third-party libraries in this folder.

We can now implement the web server, so we create a `server.js` file:

```
/* server.js */
var app = require('express')();
var http = require('http').Server(app);
var serveStatic = require('serve-static');

// Serve all files of the root directory
app.use(serveStatic('.', {'index': ['index.html']}));

// Listen on port 3000
http.listen(3000, function(){
  console.log('listening on 0.0.0.0:3000');
});
```

I will quickly guide you through the steps in the preceding code. First, we load the express package and initialize it by calling `()`. It returns the `app` reference for the web framework. In the second line, we load the internal `http` module and use the `.Server()` method to handle all requests with the Express framework. The third line loads the `serve-static` package. In the following step, we create an instance of the `serve-static` module and add it as a middleware to Express. We do this to tell Express to look for every URL for static files in the root directory and it's subfolders. The last line finally starts the server application on port `3000`.

We can now run the server by calling `node server.js` and navigate to `http://localhost:3000/` to open the client application (we will do this a little bit later).

Adding server push with WebSockets

In the title of this chapter, we referred to a *real-time* application, meaning changes in log files should be available on the client in real time/immediately. Thus, we cannot use standard `http` requests anymore because they are unidirectional from the client to the server. It's not possible to notify the client about data changes.

Real-time applications are usually implemented with a bidirectional communication between the web server and the client; thus, the WebSockets technology is exactly what we need. WebSocket is a standardized implementation of a bidirectional TCP connection for the Web. We do not want to deal with low-level protocols or compatibility issues, so we will use the awesome *Socket.IO* library, a wrapper for WebSockets with an extra compatibility layer.

 Socket.IO uses long polling to simulate a server push behavior in older browsers.

Let's add Socket.IO to our server application and package.json file:

```
npm install --save socket.io
```

We can now add the Socket.IO module to our server.js file:

```
/* server.js */
var app = require('express')();
var http = require('http').Server(app);
var serveStatic = require('serve-static');
var io = require('socket.io')(http);

// Serve all files of the root directory
app.use(serveStatic('.', {'index': ['index.html']}));

// Wait for socket connection
io.on('connection', function(socket){
  // do while a client is connected

  socket.on('disconnect', function(){
    // do when client disconnects
  });
});

http.listen(3000, function(){
    console.log('listening on 0.0.0.0:3000');
});
```

Besides initializing the socket.io module with the http server object, we implement the two event listeners: .on('connection', callback) and .on('disconnect', callback) in the preceding code. These let us execute functions whenever a client connects to the server through WebSockets and lets us cleans up everything when the client disconnects again.

We already saw that Socket.IO waits for events that are triggered by clients (such as connecting or disconnecting clients). The same principle as the .on(type, callback) function can be used to listen for custom events that are triggered by the client, for example, to transfer data from the client to the server. In the callback function, the data that was sent by the client can be accessed with the first argument. To send data from the server to the client, we use the .emit(type, data) function. This function takes an event type and a message object data as arguments.

Reading logs and pushing them to the client

Now, it's time to send some useful data through the WebSockets connection. Therefore, we add the native file system module, fs, to the application in order to read a file and push its content to the client:

```
var fs = require('fs');
var app = require('express')();
...
// Wait for socket connection
io.on('connection', function(socket){

  // Send the content of a file to the client
  var sendFile = function(name, path) {
    // Read the file
    fs.readFile(path, 'utf8', function (err, data) {
      // Emit the content of the file
      io.emit(name, data);
    });
  };

  // Wait for events on socket
  socket.on('watch', function(obj){
    sendFile(obj.name, obj.path);
  });

  socket.on('disconnect', function(){
    // do when client disconnects
  });
});
```

In the preceding example, we implement the `sendFile()` function inside the connection handler. In this function, we call the `readFile()` function. This function reads a file asynchronously and — once it is finished — pushes the content to the client via `.emit()` with an event type of the filename. Then, we set up a listener for an event watch whose message object should contain the name and path of a file and return the content of the file.

Now, we can implement a simple client that emits a watch event with the name and path of a log file and listens to an event with the name of the file. This client will look like the following code:

```
/* example/of/a/client.js */
socket.emit('watch', {
  name: 'nginx.error',
  path: '/var/log/nginx/error.log'
});

socket.on('nginx.error', function(data){
  console.log("Received: " + data);
});
```

We will use a very similar implementation later for the client. For now, let's continue with the final step.

Watching files for changes

We want to add a file watcher for every file requested by a client. This watcher should detect file changes and automatically push them to the client. Also, once a client disconnects, we need to clean up and remove all file watchers. To watch files for changes, we will use the asynchronous `watchFile()` function from the `fs` module:

```
/* server.js */
var fs = require('fs');
var app = require('express')();
var http = require('http').Server(app);
var serveStatic = require('serve-static');
var io = require('socket.io')(http);

// Serve all files from the root directory
app.use(serveStatic('.', {'index': ['index.html']}));

// Wait for socket connection
io.on('connection', function(socket){

  var watchers = [];
```

```
    // Send the content of a file to the client
    var sendFile = function(name, path) {
      // Read the file
      fs.readFile(path, 'utf8', function (err, data) {
        // Emit the content of the file
        io.emit(name, data);
      });
    };


    // Wait for events on socket
    socket.on('watch', function(obj){

      if (!watchers.hasOwnProperty(obj.name)){

        console.log("Watching " + obj.name);
        watchers[obj.name] = obj;
        sendFile(obj.name, obj.path);

        // Watch the file for changes
        fs.watchFile(obj.path, function (curr, prev) {

          sendFile(obj.name, obj.path);
        });
      }
    });

    socket.on('disconnect', function(){
      watchers.forEach(function(obj) {
        fs.unwatchFile(obj.path);
      });
    });
  });

http.listen(3000, function(){
  console.log('listening on 0.0.0.0:3000');
});
```

In the preceding code, we add a watchers array that contains all the current file watchers. This makes it easy to clean up and unwatch all the files in the disconnect handler via unwatchFile() once the connection is closed. In the connection handler, we add the watchFile() function. This function pushes the content of a file to the clients once it's changed.

These few lines are all the magic that we need to monitor files and push them to the client when they are updated, pretty cool! Also, keep in mind that we completely neglected proper error handling in this simple example.

Finally, we run the server via the `node server.js` command and open `http://localhost:3000/` for the client application.

Processing and visualizing logs on the client

In the previous section, you learned how to push the server logs from the server to the client; now, we need to organize these logs on the client, and then process and display them.

Bootstrapping a template with AngularJS and Socket.IO

Let's create a HTML page for our client application; we need to load the JavaScript libraries (D3.js, AngularJS, Socket.IO, the CSS layout Bootstrap, and all application files). Due to the usage of Socket.IO on the server side, it can be referenced on the client side with the `/socket.io/socket.io.js` pseudo location; all other third-party libraries are loaded from the `bower_components` directory.

We create the `index.html` page in the root directory of the project, add all libraries, and set up a very simple Bootstrap layout:

```html
<!-- index.html -->
<html ng-app="myApp">
  <head>
    <!-- Include 3rd party libraries -->
    <script src="bower_components/d3/d3.js" charset="UTF-
      8"></script>
    <script src="bower_components/angular/angular.js"
      charset="UTF-8"></script>

    <!-- Include Socket.io -->
    <script src="/socket.io/socket.io.js"></script>

    <!-- Include the application files -->
    <script src="src/app.js"></script>
    <link href="src/app.css" rel="stylesheet">
```

```html
<!-- Include Bootstrap -->
<link href="bower_components/bootstrap/dist/css/bootstrap.css"
  rel="stylesheet">

<!-- Include the files of the chart component -->
<script src="src/chart.js"></script>
<link href="src/chart.css" rel="stylesheet">

</head>
<body ng-controller="MainCtrl">

<div class="container">

  <nav class="navbar navbar-default">
    <!-- header goes here -->
  </nav>

  <div class="row">
    <!-- visualization goes here -->
  </div>
</div>
</body>
</html>
```

Using Socket.IO with AngularJS

As we did with D3.js, we want to integrate Socket.IO properly into the client application. In other words, encapsulate it as a service and make it injectable. Therefore, we create a new *factory* for Socket.IO in the app.js file:

```javascript
/* src/app.js */
app.factory('socket', function () {
  var socketio = io.connect();
  return socketio;
});
```

In our example, we will use the .on() method to listen for events propagated *from* the server and the .emit() method to propagate events *to* the server. To inform AngularJS about changes on the scope (outside of the AngularJS application), we need to call $scope.$apply() to trigger a digest circle that updates all scope variables. Let's write a wrapper for the .on() and .emit() functions that automatically update $rootScope. and thereby all scope variables of the application:

```javascript
/* src/app.js */
angular.module('myApp', ['myChart'])
// Socket.IO Wrapper
```

```
.factory('socket', ["$rootScope",
  function($rootScope) {
    var socketio = io.connect();
    return {
      on: function (e, callback) {
        socketio.on(e, function() {
          var args = arguments;
          $rootScope.$apply(function() {
            callback.apply(socketio, args);
          });
        });
      },
      emit: function (e, data, callback) {
        socketio.emit(e, data, function() {
          var args = arguments;
          $rootScope.$apply(function() {
            if (callback) {
              callback.apply(socketio, args);
            }
          });
        });
      }
    };
  }
])
```

The preceding implementation checks and updates the state of $rootScope on every callback of the .on() and .emit() function automatically.

Now, we can inject Socket.IO into the controller and send and receive data; let's try it:

```
/* src/app.js */
...
.controller('MainCtrl', ["$scope", "socket",
  function ($scope, socket) {
    $scope.logs = [{
      name: 'apache.access',
      path: 'var/log/apache/access.log'
    }];

    angular.forEach($scope.logs, function(log){

      socket.emit('watch', {
        name: log.name,
        path: log.path
```

```
        });

    socket.on(log.name, function(data){
        console.log("Received: " + data);

        // Now we can process the data
    });
    });
  }
]);
```

Although my browser has to struggle a little to display all the content from the Apache access log, we see that it works. This means that we receive the string of the correct data log from the server if Apache is running and the access log is updated; also, the file is reloaded. Perfect. Now, we can already think of processing the log file. Keep in mind that in a more advanced scenario, we will just transfer the small changes of the log files instead of 5 MB, of logs. It's worth mentioning that you should implement security mechanism for the HTTP connection and for the WebSockets connection as well.

Processing log files

Before we can process and display all our log files, we need to organize them and the parsing formats in the main controller of the application.

Let's create an array of logs in the controller of our application and add the processor expressions to each log type. Don't worry if the parser and map attributes seem unfamiliar to you; I will explain them right after this page:

```
/* src/app.js */
...
$scope.logs = [
{
  name: 'apache.access',
  path: 'var/log/apache/access.log',
  parser: {
    line: "\n",
    word: /[-"]/gi,
    rem: /["\[\]]/gi
  },
  map: function(d) {
    var format = d3.time.format("%d/%b/%Y:%H:%M:%S %Z");
    return {
      ip: d[0], time: +format.parse(d[2]), request: d[3], status:
        d[4], agent: d[8]
```

```
        }
      },
      data: []
    },
    {
      name: 'mysql.slow-queries',
      path: 'var/log/mysql/slow-queries.log',
      parser: {
        line: /# Time:/,
        word: /\n/gi,
        rem: /[#"\[\]]/gi
      },
      map: function(d) {
        var format = d3.time.format("%y%m%d %H:%M:%S");
        return {
          time: +format.parse(d[0]), host: d[1], query: d[2]
        }
      },
      data: []
    }
    ...
  ];
```

In the preceding code, we see that this is a very clean way to structure our log files and specify the format to parse them. The only thing missing is to actually fill the data attributes with data and change them if the log data changes. However, this is no problem with Socket.IO and our previously developed monitor server. We simply have to add watchers for every log file:

```
/* src/app.js */
angular.forEach($scope.logs, function(log){

  socket.emit('watch', {
    name: log.name,
    path: log.path
  });

  socket.on(log.name, function(data){
    console.log("Received: " + log.name);

    // Now we can really process all the data
  });
});
```

In the preceding code, we register every log file in the monitor server via the watch event; therefore, we automatically receive real-time updated data. Thanks to the watcher on the data attribute of the chart directive, the chart will be redrawn automatically when the data is updated. Now, I want to show how to process these files with the tools that we implemented in the previous chapters with two different log files. The goal is to generate a grouped array of entry objects from a big string of log entries. Let's recall the `StringParser` and the `Classifier` services that we wrote in *Chapter 5, Loading and Parsing Data*, and apply them in this example to process the log files:

```
/* src/app.js */
...
socket.on(log.name, function(data){

  // The data log as string
  var responseDataStr = data;

  // 1:
  // Parse string to an array of datum arrays
  var parsed = StringParser(responseDataStr, log.parser.line,
    log.parser.word, log.parser.rem);

  // 2:
  // Map each datum array to object
  var mapped = parsed.map(log.map);

  // 3:
  // Filter the data
  var filtered = mapped.filter(function(d){
    return !isNaN(d.time);
  });

  // 4:
  // Group the dataset by time
  var grouped = Classifier(filtered, function(d) {
    var coeff = 1000 * 60 * $scope.groupByMinutes;
    return Math.round(d.time / coeff) * coeff;
  });

  // Use the grouped data for the chart
  log.data = grouped;
});
```

Let's view the preceding code step by step:

1. We parse the log string into an array of lines where every line contains an array of strings. This means that we need to find a separator that splits the lines and a separator that splits a line into segments.

2. We map the array of segments from each line to an object. This helps us to identify the different parts of the log message (such as date, error message, ip address, and so on). We also convert the time string to a timestamp of a JavaScript `Date` object.

3. We discard all rows that don't have a valid time attribute.

4. We group the data logs by an interval of minutes. From the preceding points, point 1 is the most difficult point; therefore, I will explain it systematically with two example logs.

First, we will use a MySQL slow query log from the `var/log/mysql` directory with the following structure:

```
# Time: 141129 17:24:37
# User@Host: root[root] @ server.com [172.14.26.38]
# Query_time: 2.240000  Lock_time: 0.000000 Rows_sent: 1
  Rows_examined: 2560674
SET timestamp=1334841877;
SELECT  ...;
# Time: 141129 17:24:39
# User@Host: root[root] @ server.com [172.14.26.38]
# Query_time: 1.896000  Lock_time: 0.000000 Rows_sent: 1
  Rows_examined: 2560674
SET timestamp=1334841879;
SELECT  ...;
```

First, we can split the log string using the `/# Time:/` regular expression to generate an array of log entries:

```
Array[
  '141129 17:24:37
  # User@Host: root[root] @ server.com [172.14.26.38]
  # Query_time: 2.240000  Lock_time: 0.000000 Rows_sent: 1
    Rows_examined: 2560674
  SET timestamp=1334841877;
  SELECT  ...;',
  '141129 17:24:39
  # User@Host: root[root] @ server.com [172.14.26.38]
  # Query_time: 1.896000  Lock_time: 0.000000 Rows_sent: 1
    Rows_examined: 2560674
  SET timestamp=1334841879;
  SELECT  ...;'
];
```

Then, using the newline symbol, every single log entry can be split via the /\n/ regular expression into single segments:

```
Array[
  Array['141129 17:24:37',
  '# User@Host: root[root] @ server.com [172.14.26.38]',
  '# Query_time: 2.240000  Lock_time: 0.000000 Rows_sent: 1
    Rows_examined: 2560674',
  'SET timestamp=1334841877;',
  'SELECT  ...;'],
  Array['141129 17:24:39',
  '# User@Host: root[root] @ server.com [172.14.26.38]',
  '# Query_time: 1.896000  Lock_time: 0.000000 Rows_sent: 1
    Rows_examined: 2560674',
  'SET timestamp=1334841879;',
  'SELECT  ...;']
];
```

To make the dataset more readable, we can also remove some characters (such as # from the log entries). As a last step, we need to convert the DateTime string to a JavaScript Date Object. We can do this here by using the %y%m%d %H:%M:%S D3.js formatter. Now, we have a beautiful dataset with valid JavaScript dates. We can easily display it in a chart, for example, as a histogram.

Let's try it once more and parse a NginX error log with the following structure:

```
2014/11/29 11:13:53 [alert] 6976#8040: could not respawn worker
2014/11/29 11:14:24 [emerg] 6488#2952: unknown directive "concat"
  in /etc/nginx/conf/nginx.conf:76
```

Splitting the lines is very easy because every log entry starts on a new line; thus, we can use the /\n/ regular expression to split them:

```
Array[
  '2014/11/29 11:13:53 [alert] 6976#8040: could not respawn
    worker',
  '2014/11/29 11:14:24 [emerg] 6488#2952: unknown directive
    "concat" in /etc/nginx/conf/nginx.conf:76'
];
```

In the next step, we will divide every line into segments by splitting it with the `[` and `]` characters with the `/\[|\]/` regular expression:

```
Array[
  Array['2014/11/29 11:13:53', 'alert', '6976#8040: could not
    respawn worker'],
  Array['2014/11/29 11:14:24', 'emerg', '6488#2952: unknown
    directive "concat" in /etc/nginx/conf/nginx.conf:76']
];
```

Again, as a last step, we need to convert the `date` string into a JavaScript `Date` object; this can be done with the `%Y/%m/%d %H:%M:%S` formatter in this example.

The dashboard application

As we remember from the preceding configuration of the log files, we want to be able to display multiple charts with the built-in `ng-repeat` directive. This means that the chart directive template is just compiled once and linked multiple times. Therefore, we need to adapt the chart directives and move the initialization code for the charts from the compile phase to the link phase of the directive.

One last step needs to be done to finally see the charts of the log files, that is, to add the chart directives to the `index.html` page:

```
<!-- index.html -->
<div class="col-lg-6" ng-repeat="log in logs">
  <h3>{{ log.name }}</h3>

  <bar-chart class="chart blue" data="log.data" start-
    date="time.startDateTime" end-date="time.endDateTime" cur-
    date="time.currentDateTime">
  </bar-chart>
</div>
```

To better understand the cursor position and current zooming level, we will output the current value of the cursor and the first and last date from the current filter to the navigation bar:

```
<nav class="navbar navbar-default">
  <div class="navbar-text">
    <span>Date/Time Filter:</span>
    <span>{{ time.startDateTime | date : 'dd.MM.yyyy HH:mm'
      }}</span> -
    <span>{{ time.endDateTime | date : 'dd.MM.yyyy HH:mm'
      }}</span>
  </div>
```

```
<div class="navbar-text">
  <i>Current Date/Time: {{ time.currentDateTime | date :
    'dd.MM.yyyy HH:mm' }}</i>
</div>
</nav>
```

In the preceding code, we use the built-in AngularJS date filter to create a more readable output of the `DateTime` object.

If we now run the server and open the application, we will see four charts that are automatically updating in real time. We can see that zooming or panning in one chart also affects the current zoom and panning level in other charts. The reason for this is that all chart directives use the same reference for the `startDate` and `endDate` filter attributes as well as the `curDate` attribute. Therefore, the cursor moves and highlights in all charts simultaneously because of AngularJS' two-way-binding. Pretty neat, isn't it?

We used Bootstrap not only for it's nice visual template, but also for the built-in grid system. As a logical step, we want to make our charts responsive. This can be easily achieved by watching the window size in the chart directive and redrawing each chart when the window size changes:

```
/* src/chart.js → Chart Directive */
// Watch the window for resizing
angular.element($window).bind('resize', function(){

  // Set the width of the chart to the width of the parent element
  chart.width(element[0].parentElement.offsetWidth);
  // Redraw the chart
  chart.redraw();
});
```

Nice, now the charts adapt automatically according to the column size of the grid.

Let's open the application and take a look. The filters and cursors now play together throughout the whole application. Thanks to AngularJS, a web designer with no JavaScript knowledge can easily arrange the charts and write the HTML code for this page:

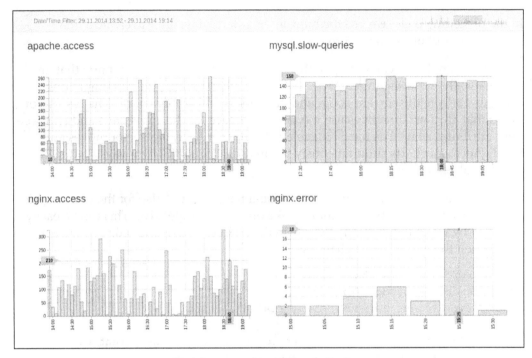

Real-time server log monitor application

Summary

In this chapter, you learned how to implement a simple monitor server that pushes data changes in real time to the client. We used Node.js because of its nonblocking I/O behavior and because of the fact that we can write the server code in JavaScript.

After installing Node.js and creating a `package.json` file for the application, we installed the `express` and `serve-static` web framework via the `npm` Node package manager.

We used the `serve-static` package to serve all the static files in the root directory of our application and added it as a middleware to `express`. This allows you to write a simple file server in less than 10 lines of code.

To implement real-time communication, we need a bidirectional connection rather than the unidirectional HTTP protocol. Therefore, we added Socket.IO, a wrapper and compatibility layer for the WebSockets protocol, a protocol for bidirectional TCP connection for the Web. With Socket.IO, we can easily receive data from a client or — the big advantage to HTTP — push data to a client.

Then, we used the `watchFile()` and `readFile()` native file system methods to asynchronously watch files for changes, read files, and push the content of files to the client.

In the end, we were able to start the server application by calling `node server.js` and open `http://localhost:3000/`, the not yet functional client.

In the second half of the chapter, we implemented the web client to visualize the server logs. To establish the bidirectional WebSockets connection, we needed to add Socket.IO to the AngularJS application. The proper way to do so is to encapsulate Socket.IO such that it can be used by the dependency injection system of AngularJS. We achieved this by wrapping it in a service.

Then, we saw how to process log files that are loaded as huge strings for our web application; we used the previously implemented `StringParser` service. The hardest point is to figure out how to properly split the string into lines of log entries and every entry into segments. In two real-world examples, we saw how to split the logs into log entry arrays with regular expression.

Later, we saw how to format the `DateTime` string of the log entries with the D3.js time formatter. Also, we organized the log file information in a configuration-like style. This helped us to clearly see where and how log files are loaded and processed.

In the end, we were very excited to put the directives in the actual page of the web client and open it in the browser. After reading all this, I am sure that you have many ideas to improve the charts, add more chart types, and more application logs.

Index

B

bar chart
  animation, creating for 187-191
Bézier curves
  about 155
  arcs, generating 164
  ellipses, drawing 159
  elliptical arcs, drawing 159, 160
  using 156-158
brush
  about 218
  custom date filter directive,
      building 222-225
  simple brush, creating 218-222
built-in SVG shapes
  URL 148

C

Canvas API 8
chart directive
  about 95
  advantages 102, 103
  building 89
  chart, drawing 99
  custom compile function, implementing 98
  e2e-testing 113, 114
  for SVG 95-97
  generalizing 103-105
  testing 105
  testing environment, setting up 106
  unit testing 110-112
chart, drawing
  about 99
  axis 99, 100
  data points, joining 101, 102
  domain 99, 100
  range 99, 100
  scale 99, 100
classifier
  testing 141
common SVG shapes
  about 148
  using 148-151
Content Delivery Network (CDN)
  URL 29

cursors
  about 198
  cursor position, labeling 203-207
  custom events 208
  self-updating cursor values,
      displaying 208-211
  simple cursor 198-201
  snappy cursors 201-203
curved lines
  drawing, with SVG path 151-153
curveto command 158
custom date format
  parsing, to JavaScript date 134
custom events
  d3.dispatch(event) 208
  dispatch.event(args) 208
  dispatch.on(event, listener) 208
  implementing 208

D

d3.entries(object) function 65
D3.js
  about 1, 11
  advantages 12
  AngularJS, working with 17
  API reference 11
  as data loading service 128
  compatibility 12
  custom directives 18, 19
  custom filters 19
  custom loading 19
  data joins 13
  debugging 12
  features 11, 12
  maintainable component 18
  parsing service 19
  performance 13
  reference link 11
  resources, finding 17
  testable component 18
  Wiki pages 11
D3.js and AngularJS integration
  about 93
  D3.js, wrapping 94, 95
  directory, organizing 93, 94

Thank you for buying
Data Visualization with D3 and AngularJS

About Packt Publishing

Packt, pronounced 'packed', published its first book, *Mastering phpMyAdmin for Effective MySQL Management*, in April 2004, and subsequently continued to specialize in publishing highly focused books on specific technologies and solutions.

Our books and publications share the experiences of your fellow IT professionals in adapting and customizing today's systems, applications, and frameworks. Our solution-based books give you the knowledge and power to customize the software and technologies you're using to get the job done. Packt books are more specific and less general than the IT books you have seen in the past. Our unique business model allows us to bring you more focused information, giving you more of what you need to know, and less of what you don't.

Packt is a modern yet unique publishing company that focuses on producing quality, cutting-edge books for communities of developers, administrators, and newbies alike. For more information, please visit our website at www.packtpub.com.

About Packt Open Source

In 2010, Packt launched two new brands, Packt Open Source and Packt Enterprise, in order to continue its focus on specialization. This book is part of the Packt Open Source brand, home to books published on software built around open source licenses, and offering information to anybody from advanced developers to budding web designers. The Open Source brand also runs Packt's Open Source Royalty Scheme, by which Packt gives a royalty to each open source project about whose software a book is sold.

Writing for Packt

We welcome all inquiries from people who are interested in authoring. Book proposals should be sent to author@packtpub.com. If your book idea is still at an early stage and you would like to discuss it first before writing a formal book proposal, then please contact us; one of our commissioning editors will get in touch with you.

We're not just looking for published authors; if you have strong technical skills but no writing experience, our experienced editors can help you develop a writing career, or simply get some additional reward for your expertise.

Mastering Web Application Development with AngularJS

ISBN: 978-1-78216-182-0   Paperback: 372 pages

Build single-page web applications using the power of AngularJS

1. Make the most out of AngularJS by understanding the AngularJS philosophy and applying it to real-life development tasks.

2. Effectively structure, write, test, and finally deploy your application.

3. Add security and optimization features to your AngularJS applications.

4. Harness the full power of AngularJS by creating your own directives.

Mastering AngularJS Directives

ISBN: 978-1-78398-158-8   Paperback: 210 pages

Develop, maintain, and test production-ready directives for any AngularJS-based application

1. Explore the options available for creating directives, by reviewing detailed explanations and real-world examples.

2. Dissect the life cycle of a directive and understand why they are the base of the AngularJS framework.

3. Discover how to create structured, maintainable, and testable directives through a step-by-step, hands-on approach to AngularJS.

Please check **www.PacktPub.com** for information on our titles

Mastering D3.js

ISBN: 978-1-78328-627-0   Paperback: 352 pages

Bring your data to life by creating and deploying complex data visualizations with D3.js

1. Create custom charts as reusable components to be integrated with existing projects.

2. Design data-driven applications with several charts interacting between them.

3. Create an analytics dashboard to display real-time data using Node and D3 with real world examples.

R Data Visualization Cookbook

ISBN: 978-1-78398-950-8   Paperback: 236 pages

Over 80 recipes to analyze data and create stunning visualizations with R

1. Create animated and interactive plots to help you communicate and explore data.

2. Utilize various R packages to generate graphs, manipulate data, and create beautiful presentations.

3. Learn to interpret data and tell a story using this step-by-step guide to data visualization.

Please check **www.PacktPub.com** for information on our titles

www.ingramcontent.com/pod-product-compliance
Lightning Source LLC
Chambersburg PA
CBHW060528060326
40690CB00017B/3418